# This Log Book Belongs To:

---------------------------------------------

---------------------------------------------

---------------------------------------------

# How To Use This Repairs Log Book

## Keeping a repairs log is useful

We recommend the use of a repairs log, which will help a system or scheme keep track of any outstanding repairs. Your system may have already have set up its own log to monitor repairs and that is fine. If you have not, then you may want to use our log sheets.

## How to use the log sheets

We hope the log sheets are easy to use, but you may also want to mark in your system's diary the date a repair is due to be completed so that you can contact the support staff promptly if something has gone wrong. Support staff can check the log book for information about what to do if this happens.
Keep some brief notes on the repairs log about how well a repair is carried out. the support staff may ask for some feedback as part of rating system.

# Repairs Log Sheet

| | |
|---|---|
| Repair Job No: | Date: 📅 |

Name of person reporting repair: 👤

Where is the fault? 🔍

Description of fault / repair required:

| Priority given: | ☐ Emergency | ☐ Routine | ☐ 5 working days |
|---|---|---|---|
| | ☐ Urgent | ☐ 24 hours | ☐ 20 working days |

Name of Company doing the work: 🏢

Name of person carrying out work: 🪪 ID

| Work Start Date: 📅 | Start Time: | am/pm |
|---|---|---|
| Work Finish Date: 📅 | Finish Time: | am/pm |

| Is a return visit needed for this job? | ☐ YES ☐ NO |
|---|---|

# Return Visit Work

| Work Start Date: 📅 | Start Time: | am/pm |
|---|---|---|
| Work Finish Date: 📅 | Finish Time: | am/pm |

| Is a return visit needed for this job? | ☐ YES ☐ NO |
|---|---|

| Work Start Date: 📅 | Start Time: | am/pm |
|---|---|---|
| Work Finish Date: 📅 | Finish Time: | am/pm |

Date repair is completed:

Notes / Comments:

# Repairs Log Sheet

| | |
|---|---|
| Repair Job No: | Date: |

Name of person reporting repair:

Where is the fault?

Description of fault / repair required:

Priority given:

- ☐ Emergency
- ☐ Urgent
- ☐ Routine
- ☐ 24 hours
- ☐ 5 working days
- ☐ 20 working days

Name of Company doing the work:

Name of person carrying out work:

| | | |
|---|---|---|
| Work Start Date: | Start Time: | am/pm |
| Work Finish Date: | Finish Time: | am/pm |

Is a return visit needed for this job?     ☐ YES  ☐ NO

# Return Visit Work

| | | |
|---|---|---|
| Work Start Date: | Start Time: | am/pm |
| Work Finish Date: | Finish Time: | am/pm |

Is a return visit needed for this job?     ☐ YES  ☐ NO

| | | |
|---|---|---|
| Work Start Date: | Start Time: | am/pm |
| Work Finish Date: | Finish Time: | am/pm |

Date repair is completed:

Notes / Comments:

# Repairs Log Sheet

| Repair Job No: | Date: | 📅 |
|---|---|---|

**Name of person reporting repair:** 👤

**Where is the fault?** 🔍

**Description of fault / repair required:**

| Priority given: | ☐ Emergency | ☐ Routine | ☐ 5 working days |
|---|---|---|---|
| | ☐ Urgent | ☐ 24 hours | ☐ 20 working days |

**Name of Company doing the work:** 🏢

**Name of person carrying out work:** 🪪

| Work Start Date: | 📅 | Start Time: | am/pm |
|---|---|---|---|
| Work Finish Date: | 📅 | Finish Time: | am/pm |

| Is a return visit needed for this job? | ☐ YES ☐ NO |
|---|---|

# Return Visit Work

| Work Start Date: | 📅 | Start Time: | am/pm |
|---|---|---|---|
| Work Finish Date: | 📅 | Finish Time: | am/pm |

| Is a return visit needed for this job? | ☐ YES ☐ NO |
|---|---|

| Work Start Date: | 📅 | Start Time: | am/pm |
|---|---|---|---|
| Work Finish Date: | 📅 | Finish Time: | am/pm |

**Date repair is completed:**

**Notes / Comments:**

# Repairs Log Sheet

| Repair Job No: | Date: |
|---|---|

Name of person reporting repair:

Where is the fault?

Description of fault / repair required:

| Priority given: | ☐ Emergency | ☐ Routine | ☐ 5 working days |
|---|---|---|---|
| | ☐ Urgent | ☐ 24 hours | ☐ 20 working days |

Name of Company doing the work:

Name of person carrying out work:

| Work Start Date: | Start Time: | am/pm |
|---|---|---|
| Work Finish Date: | Finish Time: | am/pm |

Is a return visit needed for this job?   ☐ YES ☐ NO

# Return Visit Work

| Work Start Date: | Start Time: | am/pm |
|---|---|---|
| Work Finish Date: | Finish Time: | am/pm |

Is a return visit needed for this job?   ☐ YES ☐ NO

| Work Start Date: | Start Time: | am/pm |
|---|---|---|
| Work Finish Date: | Finish Time: | am/pm |

Date repair is completed:

Notes / Comments:

# Repairs Log Sheet

| Repair Job No: | Date: 📅 |
|---|---|

Name of person reporting repair: 👤

Where is the fault? 🔍

Description of fault / repair required:

| Priority given: | ☐ Emergency | ☐ Routine | ☐ 5 working days |
|---|---|---|---|
| | ☐ Urgent | ☐ 24 hours | ☐ 20 working days |

Name of Company doing the work: 🏢

Name of person carrying out work: 🪪

| Work Start Date: 📅 | Start Time: | am/pm |
|---|---|---|
| Work Finish Date: 📅 | Finish Time: | am/pm |

Is a return visit needed for this job?　　☐ YES ☐ NO

# Return Visit Work

| Work Start Date: 📅 | Start Time: | am/pm |
|---|---|---|
| Work Finish Date: 📅 | Finish Time: | am/pm |

Is a return visit needed for this job?　　☐ YES ☐ NO

| Work Start Date: 📅 | Start Time: | am/pm |
|---|---|---|
| Work Finish Date: 📅 | Finish Time: | am/pm |

Date repair is completed:

Notes / Comments:

# Repairs Log Sheet

| Repair Job No: | Date: | 📅 |
|---|---|---|

**Name of person reporting repair:** 👤

**Where is the fault?** 🔍

**Description of fault / repair required:**

| Priority given: | ☐ Emergency | ☐ Routine | ☐ 5 working days |
|---|---|---|---|
| | ☐ Urgent | ☐ 24 hours | ☐ 20 working days |

**Name of Company doing the work:** 🏢

**Name of person carrying out work:** 🪪

| Work Start Date: | 📅 | Start Time: | am/pm |
|---|---|---|---|
| Work Finish Date: | 📅 | Finish Time: | am/pm |

Is a return visit needed for this job?  ☐ YES  ☐ NO

# Return Visit Work

| Work Start Date: | 📅 | Start Time: | am/pm |
|---|---|---|---|
| Work Finish Date: | 📅 | Finish Time: | am/pm |

Is a return visit needed for this job?  ☐ YES  ☐ NO

| Work Start Date: | 📅 | Start Time: | am/pm |
|---|---|---|---|
| Work Finish Date: | 📅 | Finish Time: | am/pm |

**Date repair is completed:**

**Notes / Comments:**

# Repairs Log Sheet

| Repair Job No: | Date: 📅 |
|---|---|

**Name of person reporting repair:** 👤

**Where is the fault?** 🔍

**Description of fault / repair required:**

| Priority given: | ☐ Emergency | ☐ Routine | ☐ 5 working days |
|---|---|---|---|
| | ☐ Urgent | ☐ 24 hours | ☐ 20 working days |

**Name of Company doing the work:** 🏢

**Name of person carrying out work:** 🆔

| Work Start Date: 📅 | Start Time: am/pm |
|---|---|
| Work Finish Date: 📅 | Finish Time: am/pm |

| Is a return visit needed for this job? | ☐ YES ☐ NO |
|---|---|

# Return Visit Work

| Work Start Date: 📅 | Start Time: am/pm |
|---|---|
| Work Finish Date: 📅 | Finish Time: am/pm |

| Is a return visit needed for this job? | ☐ YES ☐ NO |
|---|---|

| Work Start Date: 📅 | Start Time: am/pm |
|---|---|
| Work Finish Date: 📅 | Finish Time: am/pm |

**Date repair is completed:**

**Notes / Comments:**

# Repairs Log Sheet

| Repair Job No: | Date: | 📅 |

Name of person reporting repair: 👤

Where is the fault? 🔍

Description of fault / repair required:

| Priority given: | ☐ Emergency | ☐ Routine | ☐ 5 working days |
| | ☐ Urgent | ☐ 24 hours | ☐ 20 working days |

Name of Company doing the work: 🏢

Name of person carrying out work: 🪪

| Work Start Date: | 📅 | Start Time: | am/pm |
| Work Finish Date: | 📅 | Finish Time: | am/pm |

Is a return visit needed for this job?   ☐ YES ☐ NO

# Return Visit Work

| Work Start Date: | 📅 | Start Time: | am/pm |
| Work Finish Date: | 📅 | Finish Time: | am/pm |

Is a return visit needed for this job?   ☐ YES ☐ NO

| Work Start Date: | 📅 | Start Time: | am/pm |
| Work Finish Date: | 📅 | Finish Time: | am/pm |

Date repair is completed:

Notes / Comments:

# Repairs Log Sheet

| Repair Job No: | Date: | 📅 |
|---|---|---|

Name of person reporting repair: 👤

Where is the fault? 🔍

Description of fault / repair required:

| Priority given: | ☐ Emergency | ☐ Routine | ☐ 5 working days |
|---|---|---|---|
| | ☐ Urgent | ☐ 24 hours | ☐ 20 working days |

Name of Company doing the work: 🏢

Name of person carrying out work: 🪪

| Work Start Date: | 📅 | Start Time: | am/pm |
|---|---|---|---|
| Work Finish Date: | 📅 | Finish Time: | am/pm |

Is a return visit needed for this job?     ☐ YES ☐ NO

# Return Visit Work

| Work Start Date: | 📅 | Start Time: | am/pm |
|---|---|---|---|
| Work Finish Date: | 📅 | Finish Time: | am/pm |

Is a return visit needed for this job?     ☐ YES ☐ NO

| Work Start Date: | 📅 | Start Time: | am/pm |
|---|---|---|---|
| Work Finish Date: | 📅 | Finish Time: | am/pm |

Date repair is completed:

Notes / Comments:

# Repairs Log Sheet

| Repair Job No: | Date: | 📅 |
|---|---|---|

**Name of person reporting repair:** 👤

**Where is the fault?** 🔍

**Description of fault / repair required:**

| Priority given: | ☐ Emergency | ☐ Routine | ☐ 5 working days |
|---|---|---|---|
| | ☐ Urgent | ☐ 24 hours | ☐ 20 working days |

**Name of Company doing the work:** 🏢

**Name of person carrying out work:** 🪪

| Work Start Date: | 📅 | Start Time: | am/pm |
|---|---|---|---|
| Work Finish Date: | 📅 | Finish Time: | am/pm |

Is a return visit needed for this job?      ☐ YES   ☐ NO

# Return Visit Work

| Work Start Date: | 📅 | Start Time: | am/pm |
|---|---|---|---|
| Work Finish Date: | 📅 | Finish Time: | am/pm |

Is a return visit needed for this job?      ☐ YES   ☐ NO

| Work Start Date: | 📅 | Start Time: | am/pm |
|---|---|---|---|
| Work Finish Date: | 📅 | Finish Time: | am/pm |

**Date repair is completed:**

**Notes / Comments:**

# Repairs Log Sheet

| Repair Job No: | Date: | 📅 |
|---|---|---|

Name of person reporting repair: 👤

Where is the fault? 🔍

Description of fault / repair required:

| Priority given: | ☐ Emergency | ☐ Routine | ☐ 5 working days |
|---|---|---|---|
| | ☐ Urgent | ☐ 24 hours | ☐ 20 working days |

Name of Company doing the work: 🏢

Name of person carrying out work: 🪪

| Work Start Date: | 📅 | Start Time: | am/pm |
|---|---|---|---|
| Work Finish Date: | 📅 | Finish Time: | am/pm |

Is a return visit needed for this job?   ☐ YES ☐ NO

# Return Visit Work

| Work Start Date: | 📅 | Start Time: | am/pm |
|---|---|---|---|
| Work Finish Date: | 📅 | Finish Time: | am/pm |

Is a return visit needed for this job?   ☐ YES ☐ NO

| Work Start Date: | 📅 | Start Time: | am/pm |
|---|---|---|---|
| Work Finish Date: | 📅 | Finish Time: | am/pm |

Date repair is completed:

Notes / Comments:

# Repairs Log Sheet

| Repair Job No: | Date: 📅 |
|---|---|

Name of person reporting repair: 👤

Where is the fault? 🔍

Description of fault / repair required:

| Priority given: | ☐ Emergency | ☐ Routine | ☐ 5 working days |
| | ☐ Urgent | ☐ 24 hours | ☐ 20 working days |

Name of Company doing the work: 🏢

Name of person carrying out work: 🪪

| Work Start Date: 📅 | Start Time: | am/pm |
|---|---|---|
| Work Finish Date: 📅 | Finish Time: | am/pm |

Is a return visit needed for this job?  ☐ YES  ☐ NO

# Return Visit Work

| Work Start Date: 📅 | Start Time: | am/pm |
|---|---|---|
| Work Finish Date: 📅 | Finish Time: | am/pm |

Is a return visit needed for this job?  ☐ YES  ☐ NO

| Work Start Date: 📅 | Start Time: | am/pm |
|---|---|---|
| Work Finish Date: 📅 | Finish Time: | am/pm |

Date repair is completed:

Notes / Comments:

# Repairs Log Sheet

| Repair Job No: | Date: 📅 |
|---|---|

| Name of person reporting repair: 👤 |
|---|

| Where is the fault? 🔍 |
|---|

| Description of fault / repair required: |
|---|

| Priority given: | ☐ Emergency | ☐ Routine | ☐ 5 working days |
|---|---|---|---|
| | ☐ Urgent | ☐ 24 hours | ☐ 20 working days |

| Name of Company doing the work: 🏢 |
|---|

| Name of person carrying out work: 🪪 |
|---|

| Work Start Date: 📅 | Start Time: am/pm |
|---|---|
| Work Finish Date: 📅 | Finish Time: am/pm |
| Is a return visit needed for this job? | ☐ YES ☐ NO |

# Return Visit Work

| Work Start Date: 📅 | Start Time: am/pm |
|---|---|
| Work Finish Date: 📅 | Finish Time: am/pm |
| Is a return visit needed for this job? | ☐ YES ☐ NO |
| Work Start Date: 📅 | Start Time: am/pm |
| Work Finish Date: 📅 | Finish Time: am/pm |
| Date repair is completed: | |

Notes / Comments:

# Repairs Log Sheet

| | |
|---|---|
| Repair Job No: | Date: 📅 |

Name of person reporting repair: 👤

Where is the fault? 🔍

Description of fault / repair required:

| Priority given: | ☐ Emergency | ☐ Routine | ☐ 5 working days |
|---|---|---|---|
| | ☐ Urgent | ☐ 24 hours | ☐ 20 working days |

Name of Company doing the work: 🏢

Name of person carrying out work: 🪪

| Work Start Date: 📅 | Start Time: | am/pm |
|---|---|---|
| Work Finish Date: 📅 | Finish Time: | am/pm |

| Is a return visit needed for this job? | ☐ YES ☐ NO |
|---|---|

# Return Visit Work

| Work Start Date: 📅 | Start Time: | am/pm |
|---|---|---|
| Work Finish Date: 📅 | Finish Time: | am/pm |

| Is a return visit needed for this job? | ☐ YES ☐ NO |
|---|---|

| Work Start Date: 📅 | Start Time: | am/pm |
|---|---|---|
| Work Finish Date: 📅 | Finish Time: | am/pm |

Date repair is completed:

Notes / Comments: _____
_____
_____
_____
_____
_____

# Repairs Log Sheet

| Repair Job No: | Date: | 📅 |
|---|---|---|

**Name of person reporting repair:** 👤

**Where is the fault?** 🔍

**Description of fault / repair required:**

| Priority given: | ☐ Emergency | ☐ Routine | ☐ 5 working days |
|---|---|---|---|
| | ☐ Urgent | ☐ 24 hours | ☐ 20 working days |

**Name of Company doing the work:** 🏢

**Name of person carrying out work:** 🪪 ID

| Work Start Date: | 📅 | Start Time: | am/pm |
|---|---|---|---|
| Work Finish Date: | 📅 | Finish Time: | am/pm |

**Is a return visit needed for this job?**  ☐ YES ☐ NO

# Return Visit Work

| Work Start Date: | 📅 | Start Time: | am/pm |
|---|---|---|---|
| Work Finish Date: | 📅 | Finish Time: | am/pm |

**Is a return visit needed for this job?**  ☐ YES ☐ NO

| Work Start Date: | 📅 | Start Time: | am/pm |
|---|---|---|---|
| Work Finish Date: | 📅 | Finish Time: | am/pm |

**Date repair is completed:**

**Notes / Comments:**

# Repairs Log Sheet

| Repair Job No: | Date: 📅 |
|---|---|

Name of person reporting repair: 👤

Where is the fault? 🔍

Description of fault / repair required:

| Priority given: | ☐ Emergency | ☐ Routine | ☐ 5 working days |
|---|---|---|---|
| | ☐ Urgent | ☐ 24 hours | ☐ 20 working days |

Name of Company doing the work: 🏢

Name of person carrying out work: 🆔

| Work Start Date: 📅 | Start Time: | am/pm |
|---|---|---|
| Work Finish Date: 📅 | Finish Time: | am/pm |

Is a return visit needed for this job?　☐ YES　☐ NO

# Return Visit Work

| Work Start Date: 📅 | Start Time: | am/pm |
|---|---|---|
| Work Finish Date: 📅 | Finish Time: | am/pm |

Is a return visit needed for this job?　☐ YES　☐ NO

| Work Start Date: 📅 | Start Time: | am/pm |
|---|---|---|
| Work Finish Date: 📅 | Finish Time: | am/pm |

Date repair is completed:

Notes / Comments:

# Repairs Log Sheet

| Repair Job No: | Date: 📅 |
|---|---|

**Name of person reporting repair:** 👤

**Where is the fault?** 🔍

**Description of fault / repair required:**

| Priority given: | ☐ Emergency | ☐ Routine | ☐ 5 working days |
|---|---|---|---|
| | ☐ Urgent | ☐ 24 hours | ☐ 20 working days |

**Name of Company doing the work:** 🏢

**Name of person carrying out work:** 🪪

| Work Start Date: 📅 | Start Time: | am/pm |
|---|---|---|
| Work Finish Date: 📅 | Finish Time: | am/pm |

| Is a return visit needed for this job? | ☐ YES ☐ NO |
|---|---|

# Return Visit Work

| Work Start Date: 📅 | Start Time: | am/pm |
|---|---|---|
| Work Finish Date: 📅 | Finish Time: | am/pm |

| Is a return visit needed for this job? | ☐ YES ☐ NO |
|---|---|

| Work Start Date: 📅 | Start Time: | am/pm |
|---|---|---|
| Work Finish Date: 📅 | Finish Time: | am/pm |

**Date repair is completed:**

**Notes / Comments:**

# Repairs Log Sheet

| Repair Job No: | Date: 📅 |
|---|---|

Name of person reporting repair: 👤

Where is the fault? 🔍

Description of fault / repair required:

| Priority given: | ☐ Emergency | ☐ Routine | ☐ 5 working days |
|---|---|---|---|
| | ☐ Urgent | ☐ 24 hours | ☐ 20 working days |

Name of Company doing the work: 🏢

Name of person carrying out work: 🪪

| Work Start Date: 📅 | Start Time: | am/pm |
|---|---|---|
| Work Finish Date: 📅 | Finish Time: | am/pm |

| Is a return visit needed for this job? | ☐ YES ☐ NO |
|---|---|

# Return Visit Work

| Work Start Date: 📅 | Start Time: | am/pm |
|---|---|---|
| Work Finish Date: 📅 | Finish Time: | am/pm |

| Is a return visit needed for this job? | ☐ YES ☐ NO |
|---|---|

| Work Start Date: 📅 | Start Time: | am/pm |
|---|---|---|
| Work Finish Date: 📅 | Finish Time: | am/pm |

Date repair is completed:

Notes / Comments:

# Repairs Log Sheet

| Repair Job No: | Date: 📅 |
|---|---|

**Name of person reporting repair:** 👤

**Where is the fault?** 🔍

**Description of fault / repair required:**

| Priority given: | ☐ Emergency | ☐ Routine | ☐ 5 working days |
|---|---|---|---|
| | ☐ Urgent | ☐ 24 hours | ☐ 20 working days |

**Name of Company doing the work:** 🏢

**Name of person carrying out work:** 🪪

| Work Start Date: 📅 | Start Time: am/pm |
|---|---|
| Work Finish Date: 📅 | Finish Time: am/pm |

Is a return visit needed for this job?　☐ YES ☐ NO

# Return Visit Work

| Work Start Date: 📅 | Start Time: am/pm |
|---|---|
| Work Finish Date: 📅 | Finish Time: am/pm |

Is a return visit needed for this job?　☐ YES ☐ NO

| Work Start Date: 📅 | Start Time: am/pm |
|---|---|
| Work Finish Date: 📅 | Finish Time: am/pm |

Date repair is completed:

Notes / Comments:

# Repairs Log Sheet

| | |
|---|---|
| Repair Job No: | Date: |

Name of person reporting repair:

Where is the fault?

Description of fault / repair required:

| Priority given: | ☐ Emergency | ☐ Routine | ☐ 5 working days |
|---|---|---|---|
| | ☐ Urgent | ☐ 24 hours | ☐ 20 working days |

Name of Company doing the work:

Name of person carrying out work:

| Work Start Date: | Start Time: | am/pm |
|---|---|---|
| Work Finish Date: | Finish Time: | am/pm |

Is a return visit needed for this job?     ☐ YES  ☐ NO

# Return Visit Work

| Work Start Date: | Start Time: | am/pm |
|---|---|---|
| Work Finish Date: | Finish Time: | am/pm |

Is a return visit needed for this job?     ☐ YES  ☐ NO

| Work Start Date: | Start Time: | am/pm |
|---|---|---|
| Work Finish Date: | Finish Time: | am/pm |

Date repair is completed:

Notes / Comments:

# Repairs Log Sheet

| Repair Job No: | Date: | 📅 |
|---|---|---|

Name of person reporting repair: 👤

Where is the fault? 🔍

Description of fault / repair required:

| Priority given: | ☐ Emergency | ☐ Routine | ☐ 5 working days |
|---|---|---|---|
| | ☐ Urgent | ☐ 24 hours | ☐ 20 working days |

Name of Company doing the work: 🏢

Name of person carrying out work: 🪪ID

| Work Start Date: | 📅 | Start Time: | am/pm |
|---|---|---|---|
| Work Finish Date: | 📅 | Finish Time: | am/pm |

Is a return visit needed for this job?   ☐ YES ☐ NO

# Return Visit Work

| Work Start Date: | 📅 | Start Time: | am/pm |
|---|---|---|---|
| Work Finish Date: | 📅 | Finish Time: | am/pm |

Is a return visit needed for this job?   ☐ YES ☐ NO

| Work Start Date: | 📅 | Start Time: | am/pm |
|---|---|---|---|
| Work Finish Date: | 📅 | Finish Time: | am/pm |

Date repair is completed:

Notes / Comments:

# Repairs Log Sheet

| Repair Job No: | Date: | |
|---|---|---|

Name of person reporting repair:

Where is the fault?

Description of fault / repair required:

| Priority given: | ☐ Emergency | ☐ Routine | ☐ 5 working days |
|---|---|---|---|
| | ☐ Urgent | ☐ 24 hours | ☐ 20 working days |

Name of Company doing the work:

Name of person carrying out work:

| Work Start Date: | | Start Time: | am/pm |
|---|---|---|---|
| Work Finish Date: | | Finish Time: | am/pm |

| Is a return visit needed for this job? | ☐ YES ☐ NO |
|---|---|

# Return Visit Work

| Work Start Date: | | Start Time: | am/pm |
|---|---|---|---|
| Work Finish Date: | | Finish Time: | am/pm |

| Is a return visit needed for this job? | ☐ YES ☐ NO |
|---|---|

| Work Start Date: | | Start Time: | am/pm |
|---|---|---|---|
| Work Finish Date: | | Finish Time: | am/pm |

Date repair is completed:

Notes / Comments:

# Repairs Log Sheet

| Repair Job No: | Date: 📅 |
|---|---|

| Name of person reporting repair: 👤 |
|---|

| Where is the fault? 🔍 |
|---|

| Description of fault / repair required: |
|---|

| Priority given: | ☐ Emergency | ☐ Routine | ☐ 5 working days |
|---|---|---|---|
| | ☐ Urgent | ☐ 24 hours | ☐ 20 working days |

| Name of Company doing the work: 🏢 |
|---|

| Name of person carrying out work: 🪪 |
|---|

| Work Start Date: 📅 | Start Time: | am/pm |
|---|---|---|
| Work Finish Date: 📅 | Finish Time: | am/pm |

| Is a return visit needed for this job? | ☐ YES ☐ NO |
|---|---|

# Return Visit Work

| Work Start Date: 📅 | Start Time: | am/pm |
|---|---|---|
| Work Finish Date: 📅 | Finish Time: | am/pm |

| Is a return visit needed for this job? | ☐ YES ☐ NO |
|---|---|

| Work Start Date: 📅 | Start Time: | am/pm |
|---|---|---|
| Work Finish Date: 📅 | Finish Time: | am/pm |

| Date repair is completed: |
|---|

Notes / Comments:

# Repairs Log Sheet

| Repair Job No: | Date: |
|---|---|

Name of person reporting repair:

Where is the fault?

Description of fault / repair required:

| Priority given: | ☐ Emergency | ☐ Routine | ☐ 5 working days |
|---|---|---|---|
| | ☐ Urgent | ☐ 24 hours | ☐ 20 working days |

Name of Company doing the work:

Name of person carrying out work:

| Work Start Date: | Start Time: | am/pm |
|---|---|---|
| Work Finish Date: | Finish Time: | am/pm |

| Is a return visit needed for this job? | ☐ YES ☐ NO |
|---|---|

# Return Visit Work

| Work Start Date: | Start Time: | am/pm |
|---|---|---|
| Work Finish Date: | Finish Time: | am/pm |

| Is a return visit needed for this job? | ☐ YES ☐ NO |
|---|---|

| Work Start Date: | Start Time: | am/pm |
|---|---|---|
| Work Finish Date: | Finish Time: | am/pm |

Date repair is completed:

Notes / Comments:

# Repairs Log Sheet

| Repair Job No: | Date: | 📅 |
|---|---|---|

Name of person reporting repair: 👤

Where is the fault? 🔍

Description of fault / repair required:

| Priority given: | ☐ Emergency | ☐ Routine | ☐ 5 working days |
|---|---|---|---|
| | ☐ Urgent | ☐ 24 hours | ☐ 20 working days |

Name of Company doing the work: 🏢

Name of person carrying out work: 📋

| Work Start Date: | 📅 | Start Time: | am/pm |
|---|---|---|---|
| Work Finish Date: | 📅 | Finish Time: | am/pm |

Is a return visit needed for this job? ☐ YES ☐ NO

# Return Visit Work

| Work Start Date: | 📅 | Start Time: | am/pm |
|---|---|---|---|
| Work Finish Date: | 📅 | Finish Time: | am/pm |

Is a return visit needed for this job? ☐ YES ☐ NO

| Work Start Date: | 📅 | Start Time: | am/pm |
|---|---|---|---|
| Work Finish Date: | 📅 | Finish Time: | am/pm |

Date repair is completed:

Notes / Comments:

# Repairs Log Sheet

| Repair Job No: | Date: | 📅 |
|---|---|---|

**Name of person reporting repair:** 👤

**Where is the fault?** 🔍

**Description of fault / repair required:**

| Priority given: | ☐ Emergency | ☐ Routine | ☐ 5 working days |
|---|---|---|---|
| | ☐ Urgent | ☐ 24 hours | ☐ 20 working days |

**Name of Company doing the work:** 🏢

**Name of person carrying out work:** 🪪

| Work Start Date: | 📅 | Start Time: | am/pm |
|---|---|---|---|
| Work Finish Date: | 📅 | Finish Time: | am/pm |

Is a return visit needed for this job?     ☐ YES   ☐ NO

# Return Visit Work

| Work Start Date: | 📅 | Start Time: | am/pm |
|---|---|---|---|
| Work Finish Date: | 📅 | Finish Time: | am/pm |

Is a return visit needed for this job?     ☐ YES   ☐ NO

| Work Start Date: | 📅 | Start Time: | am/pm |
|---|---|---|---|
| Work Finish Date: | 📅 | Finish Time: | am/pm |

Date repair is completed:

**Notes / Comments:**

# Repairs Log Sheet

| Repair Job No: | Date: 📅 |
|---|---|

Name of person reporting repair: 👤

Where is the fault? 🔍

Description of fault / repair required:

| Priority given: | ☐ Emergency | ☐ Routine | ☐ 5 working days |
|---|---|---|---|
| | ☐ Urgent | ☐ 24 hours | ☐ 20 working days |

Name of Company doing the work: 🏢

Name of person carrying out work: 🪪 ID

| Work Start Date: 📅 | Start Time: am/pm |
|---|---|
| Work Finish Date: 📅 | Finish Time: am/pm |

Is a return visit needed for this job?　　☐　YES　☐　NO

# Return Visit Work

| Work Start Date: 📅 | Start Time: am/pm |
|---|---|
| Work Finish Date: 📅 | Finish Time: am/pm |

Is a return visit needed for this job?　　☐　YES　☐　NO

| Work Start Date: 📅 | Start Time: am/pm |
|---|---|
| Work Finish Date: 📅 | Finish Time: am/pm |

Date repair is completed:

Notes / Comments:

# Repairs Log Sheet

| Repair Job No: | Date: |
|---|---|

Name of person reporting repair:

Where is the fault?

Description of fault / repair required:

| Priority given: | ☐ Emergency | ☐ Routine | ☐ 5 working days |
|---|---|---|---|
| | ☐ Urgent | ☐ 24 hours | ☐ 20 working days |

Name of Company doing the work:

Name of person carrying out work:

| Work Start Date: | Start Time: | am/pm |
|---|---|---|
| Work Finish Date: | Finish Time: | am/pm |

Is a return visit needed for this job?     ☐ YES  ☐ NO

# Return Visit Work

| Work Start Date: | Start Time: | am/pm |
|---|---|---|
| Work Finish Date: | Finish Time: | am/pm |

Is a return visit needed for this job?     ☐ YES  ☐ NO

| Work Start Date: | Start Time: | am/pm |
|---|---|---|
| Work Finish Date: | Finish Time: | am/pm |

Date repair is completed:

Notes / Comments:

# Repairs Log Sheet

| Repair Job No: | Date: | 📅 |
|---|---|---|

Name of person reporting repair: 👤

Where is the fault? 🔍

Description of fault / repair required:

| Priority given: | ☐ Emergency | ☐ Routine | ☐ 5 working days |
|---|---|---|---|
| | ☐ Urgent | ☐ 24 hours | ☐ 20 working days |

Name of Company doing the work: 🏢

Name of person carrying out work: 🪪

| Work Start Date: | 📅 | Start Time: | am/pm |
|---|---|---|---|
| Work Finish Date: | 📅 | Finish Time: | am/pm |

Is a return visit needed for this job?    ☐ YES  ☐ NO

# Return Visit Work

| Work Start Date: | 📅 | Start Time: | am/pm |
|---|---|---|---|
| Work Finish Date: | 📅 | Finish Time: | am/pm |

Is a return visit needed for this job?    ☐ YES  ☐ NO

| Work Start Date: | 📅 | Start Time: | am/pm |
|---|---|---|---|
| Work Finish Date: | 📅 | Finish Time: | am/pm |

Date repair is completed:

Notes / Comments:

# Repairs Log Sheet

| Repair Job No: | Date: | 📅 |
|---|---|---|

**Name of person reporting repair:** 👤

**Where is the fault?** 🔍

**Description of fault / repair required:**

| Priority given: | ☐ Emergency | ☐ Routine | ☐ 5 working days |
|---|---|---|---|
| | ☐ Urgent | ☐ 24 hours | ☐ 20 working days |

**Name of Company doing the work:** 🏢

**Name of person carrying out work:** 🪪

| Work Start Date: | 📅 | Start Time: | am/pm |
|---|---|---|---|
| Work Finish Date: | 📅 | Finish Time: | am/pm |

| Is a return visit needed for this job? | ☐ YES ☐ NO |
|---|---|

# Return Visit Work

| Work Start Date: | 📅 | Start Time: | am/pm |
|---|---|---|---|
| Work Finish Date: | 📅 | Finish Time: | am/pm |

| Is a return visit needed for this job? | ☐ YES ☐ NO |
|---|---|

| Work Start Date: | 📅 | Start Time: | am/pm |
|---|---|---|---|
| Work Finish Date: | 📅 | Finish Time: | am/pm |

**Date repair is completed:**

**Notes / Comments:**

# Repairs Log Sheet

| Repair Job No: | Date: | 📅 |
|---|---|---|

| Name of person reporting repair: | 👤 |
|---|---|

| Where is the fault? | 🔍 |
|---|---|

Description of fault / repair required:

| Priority given: | ☐ Emergency | ☐ Routine | ☐ 5 working days |
|---|---|---|---|
| | ☐ Urgent | ☐ 24 hours | ☐ 20 working days |

| Name of Company doing the work: | 🏢 |
|---|---|

| Name of person carrying out work: | 🪪 ID |
|---|---|

| Work Start Date: | 📅 | Start Time: | am/pm |
|---|---|---|---|
| Work Finish Date: | 📅 | Finish Time: | am/pm |

| Is a return visit needed for this job? | ☐ YES ☐ NO |
|---|---|

# Return Visit Work

| Work Start Date: | 📅 | Start Time: | am/pm |
|---|---|---|---|
| Work Finish Date: | 📅 | Finish Time: | am/pm |

| Is a return visit needed for this job? | ☐ YES ☐ NO |
|---|---|

| Work Start Date: | 📅 | Start Time: | am/pm |
|---|---|---|---|
| Work Finish Date: | 📅 | Finish Time: | am/pm |

Date repair is completed:

Notes / Comments:

# Repairs Log Sheet

| Repair Job No: | Date: |
|---|---|

**Name of person reporting repair:**

**Where is the fault?**

**Description of fault / repair required:**

| Priority given: | ☐ Emergency | ☐ Routine | ☐ 5 working days |
|---|---|---|---|
| | ☐ Urgent | ☐ 24 hours | ☐ 20 working days |

**Name of Company doing the work:**

**Name of person carrying out work:**

| Work Start Date: | Start Time: | am/pm |
|---|---|---|
| Work Finish Date: | Finish Time: | am/pm |

| Is a return visit needed for this job? | ☐ YES ☐ NO |
|---|---|

# Return Visit Work

| Work Start Date: | Start Time: | am/pm |
|---|---|---|
| Work Finish Date: | Finish Time: | am/pm |

| Is a return visit needed for this job? | ☐ YES ☐ NO |
|---|---|

| Work Start Date: | Start Time: | am/pm |
|---|---|---|
| Work Finish Date: | Finish Time: | am/pm |

**Date repair is completed:**

**Notes / Comments:**

# Repairs Log Sheet

| | |
|---|---|
| Repair Job No: | Date: |

Name of person reporting repair:

Where is the fault?

Description of fault / repair required:

Priority given:
- ☐ Emergency ☐ Routine ☐ 5 working days
- ☐ Urgent ☐ 24 hours ☐ 20 working days

Name of Company doing the work:

Name of person carrying out work:

| | | | |
|---|---|---|---|
| Work Start Date: | | Start Time: | am/pm |
| Work Finish Date: | | Finish Time: | am/pm |

Is a return visit needed for this job?  ☐ YES ☐ NO

# Return Visit Work

| | | | |
|---|---|---|---|
| Work Start Date: | | Start Time: | am/pm |
| Work Finish Date: | | Finish Time: | am/pm |

Is a return visit needed for this job?  ☐ YES ☐ NO

| | | | |
|---|---|---|---|
| Work Start Date: | | Start Time: | am/pm |
| Work Finish Date: | | Finish Time: | am/pm |

Date repair is completed:

Notes / Comments:

# Repairs Log Sheet

| Repair Job No: | Date: 📅 |
|---|---|

Name of person reporting repair: 👤

Where is the fault? 🔍

Description of fault / repair required:

| Priority given: | ☐ Emergency | ☐ Routine | ☐ 5 working days |
|---|---|---|---|
| | ☐ Urgent | ☐ 24 hours | ☐ 20 working days |

Name of Company doing the work: 🏢

Name of person carrying out work: 🪪

| Work Start Date: 📅 | Start Time: | am/pm |
|---|---|---|
| Work Finish Date: 📅 | Finish Time: | am/pm |

Is a return visit needed for this job? ☐ YES ☐ NO

# Return Visit Work

| Work Start Date: 📅 | Start Time: | am/pm |
|---|---|---|
| Work Finish Date: 📅 | Finish Time: | am/pm |

Is a return visit needed for this job? ☐ YES ☐ NO

| Work Start Date: 📅 | Start Time: | am/pm |
|---|---|---|
| Work Finish Date: 📅 | Finish Time: | am/pm |

Date repair is completed:

Notes / Comments:

# Repairs Log Sheet

| Repair Job No: | Date: | 📅 |
|---|---|---|

Name of person reporting repair: 👤

Where is the fault? 🔍

Description of fault / repair required:

| Priority given: | ☐ Emergency | ☐ Routine | ☐ 5 working days |
|---|---|---|---|
| | ☐ Urgent | ☐ 24 hours | ☐ 20 working days |

Name of Company doing the work: 🏢

Name of person carrying out work: 🪪 ID

| Work Start Date: | 📅 | Start Time: | am/pm |
|---|---|---|---|
| Work Finish Date: | 📅 | Finish Time: | am/pm |

Is a return visit needed for this job?　　☐ YES　☐ NO

# Return Visit Work

| Work Start Date: | 📅 | Start Time: | am/pm |
|---|---|---|---|
| Work Finish Date: | 📅 | Finish Time: | am/pm |

Is a return visit needed for this job?　　☐ YES　☐ NO

| Work Start Date: | 📅 | Start Time: | am/pm |
|---|---|---|---|
| Work Finish Date: | 📅 | Finish Time: | am/pm |

Date repair is completed:

Notes / Comments:

# Repairs Log Sheet

| Repair Job No: | Date: |
|---|---|

Name of person reporting repair:

Where is the fault?

Description of fault / repair required:

| Priority given: | ☐ Emergency | ☐ Routine | ☐ 5 working days |
|---|---|---|---|
| | ☐ Urgent | ☐ 24 hours | ☐ 20 working days |

Name of Company doing the work:

Name of person carrying out work:

| Work Start Date: | Start Time: | am/pm |
|---|---|---|
| Work Finish Date: | Finish Time: | am/pm |

Is a return visit needed for this job?  ☐ YES  ☐ NO

# Return Visit Work

| Work Start Date: | Start Time: | am/pm |
|---|---|---|
| Work Finish Date: | Finish Time: | am/pm |

Is a return visit needed for this job?  ☐ YES  ☐ NO

| Work Start Date: | Start Time: | am/pm |
|---|---|---|
| Work Finish Date: | Finish Time: | am/pm |

Date repair is completed:

Notes / Comments:

# Repairs Log Sheet

| Repair Job No: | Date: | 📅 |
|---|---|---|

| Name of person reporting repair: | 👤 |
|---|---|

| Where is the fault? | 🔍 |
|---|---|

Description of fault / repair required:

| Priority given: | ☐ Emergency | ☐ Routine | ☐ 5 working days |
|---|---|---|---|
| | ☐ Urgent | ☐ 24 hours | ☐ 20 working days |

| Name of Company doing the work: | 🏢 |
|---|---|

| Name of person carrying out work: | 🪪 ID |
|---|---|

| Work Start Date: | 📅 | Start Time: | am/pm |
|---|---|---|---|
| Work Finish Date: | 📅 | Finish Time: | am/pm |

| Is a return visit needed for this job? | ☐ YES ☐ NO |
|---|---|

# Return Visit Work

| Work Start Date: | 📅 | Start Time: | am/pm |
|---|---|---|---|
| Work Finish Date: | 📅 | Finish Time: | am/pm |

| Is a return visit needed for this job? | ☐ YES ☐ NO |
|---|---|

| Work Start Date: | 📅 | Start Time: | am/pm |
|---|---|---|---|
| Work Finish Date: | 📅 | Finish Time: | am/pm |

Date repair is completed:

Notes / Comments:

# Repairs Log Sheet

| Repair Job No: | Date: | 📅 |
|---|---|---|

Name of person reporting repair: 👤

Where is the fault? 🔍

Description of fault / repair required:

| Priority given: | ☐ Emergency | ☐ Routine | ☐ 5 working days |
|---|---|---|---|
| | ☐ Urgent | ☐ 24 hours | ☐ 20 working days |

Name of Company doing the work: 🏢

Name of person carrying out work: 🪪

| Work Start Date: | 📅 | Start Time: | am/pm |
|---|---|---|---|
| Work Finish Date: | 📅 | Finish Time: | am/pm |

Is a return visit needed for this job? ☐ YES ☐ NO

# Return Visit Work

| Work Start Date: | 📅 | Start Time: | am/pm |
|---|---|---|---|
| Work Finish Date: | 📅 | Finish Time: | am/pm |

Is a return visit needed for this job? ☐ YES ☐ NO

| Work Start Date: | 📅 | Start Time: | am/pm |
|---|---|---|---|
| Work Finish Date: | 📅 | Finish Time: | am/pm |

Date repair is completed:

Notes / Comments:

# Repairs Log Sheet

| Repair Job No: | Date: | 📅 |
|---|---|---|

| Name of person reporting repair: | 👤 |
|---|---|

| Where is the fault? | 🔍 |
|---|---|

**Description of fault / repair required:**

| Priority given: | ☐ Emergency | ☐ Routine | ☐ 5 working days |
|---|---|---|---|
| | ☐ Urgent | ☐ 24 hours | ☐ 20 working days |

| Name of Company doing the work: | 🏢 |
|---|---|

| Name of person carrying out work: | 🆔 |
|---|---|

| Work Start Date: | 📅 | Start Time: | am/pm |
|---|---|---|---|
| Work Finish Date: | 📅 | Finish Time: | am/pm |

| Is a return visit needed for this job? | ☐ YES ☐ NO |
|---|---|

# Return Visit Work

| Work Start Date: | 📅 | Start Time: | am/pm |
|---|---|---|---|
| Work Finish Date: | 📅 | Finish Time: | am/pm |

| Is a return visit needed for this job? | ☐ YES ☐ NO |
|---|---|

| Work Start Date: | 📅 | Start Time: | am/pm |
|---|---|---|---|
| Work Finish Date: | 📅 | Finish Time: | am/pm |

Date repair is completed:

Notes / Comments:

# Repairs Log Sheet

| | |
|---|---|
| Repair Job No: | Date: 📅 |

Name of person reporting repair: 👤

Where is the fault? 🔍

Description of fault / repair required:

| Priority given: | ☐ Emergency | ☐ Routine | ☐ 5 working days |
|---|---|---|---|
| | ☐ Urgent | ☐ 24 hours | ☐ 20 working days |

Name of Company doing the work: 🏢

Name of person carrying out work: 🪪

| Work Start Date: 📅 | Start Time: | am/pm |
|---|---|---|
| Work Finish Date: 📅 | Finish Time: | am/pm |

| Is a return visit needed for this job? | ☐ YES ☐ NO |
|---|---|

# Return Visit Work

| Work Start Date: 📅 | Start Time: | am/pm |
|---|---|---|
| Work Finish Date: 📅 | Finish Time: | am/pm |

| Is a return visit needed for this job? | ☐ YES ☐ NO |
|---|---|

| Work Start Date: 📅 | Start Time: | am/pm |
|---|---|---|
| Work Finish Date: 📅 | Finish Time: | am/pm |

Date repair is completed:

Notes / Comments:

# Repairs Log Sheet

| Repair Job No: | Date: 📅 |
|---|---|

**Name of person reporting repair:** 👤

**Where is the fault?** 🔍

**Description of fault / repair required:**

| Priority given: | ☐ Emergency<br>☐ Urgent | ☐ Routine<br>☐ 24 hours | ☐ 5 working days<br>☐ 20 working days |
|---|---|---|---|

**Name of Company doing the work:** 🏢

**Name of person carrying out work:** 🪪

| Work Start Date: 📅 | Start Time: | am/pm |
|---|---|---|
| Work Finish Date: 📅 | Finish Time: | am/pm |

| Is a return visit needed for this job? | ☐ YES ☐ NO |
|---|---|

# Return Visit Work

| Work Start Date: 📅 | Start Time: | am/pm |
|---|---|---|
| Work Finish Date: 📅 | Finish Time: | am/pm |

| Is a return visit needed for this job? | ☐ YES ☐ NO |
|---|---|

| Work Start Date: 📅 | Start Time: | am/pm |
|---|---|---|
| Work Finish Date: 📅 | Finish Time: | am/pm |

**Date repair is completed:**

**Notes / Comments:**

# Repairs Log Sheet

| Repair Job No: | Date: |
|---|---|

Name of person reporting repair:

Where is the fault?

Description of fault / repair required:

| Priority given: | ☐ Emergency | ☐ Routine | ☐ 5 working days |
|---|---|---|---|
| | ☐ Urgent | ☐ 24 hours | ☐ 20 working days |

Name of Company doing the work:

Name of person carrying out work:

| Work Start Date: | Start Time: | am/pm |
|---|---|---|
| Work Finish Date: | Finish Time: | am/pm |

Is a return visit needed for this job?　☐ YES ☐ NO

# Return Visit Work

| Work Start Date: | Start Time: | am/pm |
|---|---|---|
| Work Finish Date: | Finish Time: | am/pm |

Is a return visit needed for this job?　☐ YES ☐ NO

| Work Start Date: | Start Time: | am/pm |
|---|---|---|
| Work Finish Date: | Finish Time: | am/pm |

Date repair is completed:

Notes / Comments:

# Repairs Log Sheet

| Repair Job No: | Date: | 📅 |
| --- | --- | --- |

| Name of person reporting repair: | 👤 |
| --- | --- |

| Where is the fault? | 🔍 |
| --- | --- |

| Description of fault / repair required: |
| --- |

| Priority given: | ☐ Emergency | ☐ Routine | ☐ 5 working days |
| --- | --- | --- | --- |
| | ☐ Urgent | ☐ 24 hours | ☐ 20 working days |

| Name of Company doing the work: | 🏢 |
| --- | --- |

| Name of person carrying out work: | 🪪 |
| --- | --- |

| Work Start Date: | 📅 | Start Time: | am/pm |
| --- | --- | --- | --- |
| Work Finish Date: | 📅 | Finish Time: | am/pm |

| Is a return visit needed for this job? | ☐ YES ☐ NO |
| --- | --- |

# Return Visit Work

| Work Start Date: | 📅 | Start Time: | am/pm |
| --- | --- | --- | --- |
| Work Finish Date: | 📅 | Finish Time: | am/pm |

| Is a return visit needed for this job? | ☐ YES ☐ NO |
| --- | --- |

| Work Start Date: | 📅 | Start Time: | am/pm |
| --- | --- | --- | --- |
| Work Finish Date: | 📅 | Finish Time: | am/pm |

| Date repair is completed: |
| --- |

Notes / Comments:

# Repairs Log Sheet

| Repair Job No: | Date: 📅 |
|---|---|

Name of person reporting repair: 👤

Where is the fault? 🔍

Description of fault / repair required:

| Priority given: | ☐ Emergency | ☐ Routine | ☐ 5 working days |
|---|---|---|---|
| | ☐ Urgent | ☐ 24 hours | ☐ 20 working days |

Name of Company doing the work: 🏢

Name of person carrying out work: 🪪

| Work Start Date: 📅 | Start Time: am/pm |
|---|---|
| Work Finish Date: 📅 | Finish Time: am/pm |

Is a return visit needed for this job?    ☐ YES   ☐ NO

# Return Visit Work

| Work Start Date: 📅 | Start Time: am/pm |
|---|---|
| Work Finish Date: 📅 | Finish Time: am/pm |

Is a return visit needed for this job?    ☐ YES   ☐ NO

| Work Start Date: 📅 | Start Time: am/pm |
|---|---|
| Work Finish Date: 📅 | Finish Time: am/pm |

Date repair is completed:

Notes / Comments:

# Repairs Log Sheet

| Repair Job No: | Date: | 📅 |
|---|---|---|

Name of person reporting repair: 👤

Where is the fault? 🔍

Description of fault / repair required:

| Priority given: | ☐ Emergency | ☐ Routine | ☐ 5 working days |
|---|---|---|---|
| | ☐ Urgent | ☐ 24 hours | ☐ 20 working days |

Name of Company doing the work: 🏢

Name of person carrying out work: 🪪

| Work Start Date: | 📅 | Start Time: | am/pm |
|---|---|---|---|
| Work Finish Date: | 📅 | Finish Time: | am/pm |

Is a return visit needed for this job?    ☐ YES  ☐ NO

# Return Visit Work

| Work Start Date: | 📅 | Start Time: | am/pm |
|---|---|---|---|
| Work Finish Date: | 📅 | Finish Time: | am/pm |

Is a return visit needed for this job?    ☐ YES  ☐ NO

| Work Start Date: | 📅 | Start Time: | am/pm |
|---|---|---|---|
| Work Finish Date: | 📅 | Finish Time: | am/pm |

Date repair is completed:

Notes / Comments:

# Repairs Log Sheet

| Repair Job No: | Date: | 📅 |
|---|---|---|

**Name of person reporting repair:** 👤

**Where is the fault?** 🔍

**Description of fault / repair required:**

| Priority given: | ☐ Emergency | ☐ Routine | ☐ 5 working days |
|---|---|---|---|
| | ☐ Urgent | ☐ 24 hours | ☐ 20 working days |

**Name of Company doing the work:** 🏢

**Name of person carrying out work:** 🪪

| Work Start Date: | 📅 | Start Time: | am/pm |
|---|---|---|---|
| Work Finish Date: | 📅 | Finish Time: | am/pm |

| Is a return visit needed for this job? | ☐ YES ☐ NO |
|---|---|

# Return Visit Work

| Work Start Date: | 📅 | Start Time: | am/pm |
|---|---|---|---|
| Work Finish Date: | 📅 | Finish Time: | am/pm |

| Is a return visit needed for this job? | ☐ YES ☐ NO |
|---|---|

| Work Start Date: | 📅 | Start Time: | am/pm |
|---|---|---|---|
| Work Finish Date: | 📅 | Finish Time: | am/pm |

**Date repair is completed:**

**Notes / Comments:**

# Repairs Log Sheet

| Repair Job No: | Date: | 📅 |
|---|---|---|

Name of person reporting repair: 👤

Where is the fault? 🔍

Description of fault / repair required:

| Priority given: | ☐ Emergency | ☐ Routine | ☐ 5 working days |
|---|---|---|---|
| | ☐ Urgent | ☐ 24 hours | ☐ 20 working days |

Name of Company doing the work: 🏢

Name of person carrying out work: 🪪

| Work Start Date: | 📅 | Start Time: | am/pm |
|---|---|---|---|
| Work Finish Date: | 📅 | Finish Time: | am/pm |

| Is a return visit needed for this job? | ☐ YES ☐ NO |
|---|---|

# Return Visit Work

| Work Start Date: | 📅 | Start Time: | am/pm |
|---|---|---|---|
| Work Finish Date: | 📅 | Finish Time: | am/pm |

| Is a return visit needed for this job? | ☐ YES ☐ NO |
|---|---|

| Work Start Date: | 📅 | Start Time: | am/pm |
|---|---|---|---|
| Work Finish Date: | 📅 | Finish Time: | am/pm |

Date repair is completed:

Notes / Comments:

# Repairs Log Sheet

| Repair Job No: | Date: | 📅 |
|---|---|---|

Name of person reporting repair: 👤

Where is the fault? 🔍

Description of fault / repair required:

| Priority given: | ☐ Emergency | ☐ Routine | ☐ 5 working days |
|---|---|---|---|
| | ☐ Urgent | ☐ 24 hours | ☐ 20 working days |

Name of Company doing the work: 🏢

Name of person carrying out work: 🆔

| Work Start Date: | 📅 | Start Time: | am/pm |
|---|---|---|---|
| Work Finish Date: | 📅 | Finish Time: | am/pm |

Is a return visit needed for this job?  ☐ YES  ☐ NO

# Return Visit Work

| Work Start Date: | 📅 | Start Time: | am/pm |
|---|---|---|---|
| Work Finish Date: | 📅 | Finish Time: | am/pm |

Is a return visit needed for this job?  ☐ YES  ☐ NO

| Work Start Date: | 📅 | Start Time: | am/pm |
|---|---|---|---|
| Work Finish Date: | 📅 | Finish Time: | am/pm |

Date repair is completed:

Notes / Comments:

# Repairs Log Sheet

| Repair Job No: | Date: | 📅 |
|---|---|---|

**Name of person reporting repair:** 👤

**Where is the fault?** 🔍

**Description of fault / repair required:**

| Priority given: | ☐ Emergency | ☐ Routine | ☐ 5 working days |
|---|---|---|---|
| | ☐ Urgent | ☐ 24 hours | ☐ 20 working days |

**Name of Company doing the work:** 🏢

**Name of person carrying out work:** 🪪

| Work Start Date: | 📅 | Start Time: | am/pm |
|---|---|---|---|
| Work Finish Date: | 📅 | Finish Time: | am/pm |

Is a return visit needed for this job?     ☐ YES  ☐ NO

# Return Visit Work

| Work Start Date: | 📅 | Start Time: | am/pm |
|---|---|---|---|
| Work Finish Date: | 📅 | Finish Time: | am/pm |

Is a return visit needed for this job?     ☐ YES  ☐ NO

| Work Start Date: | 📅 | Start Time: | am/pm |
|---|---|---|---|
| Work Finish Date: | 📅 | Finish Time: | am/pm |

Date repair is completed:

---

**Notes / Comments:**

_____

_____

_____

_____

_____

# Repairs Log Sheet

| Repair Job No: | Date: | 📅 |
|---|---|---|

Name of person reporting repair: 👤

Where is the fault? 🔍

Description of fault / repair required:

Priority given:

| | ☐ Emergency | ☐ Routine | ☐ 5 working days |
|---|---|---|---|
| | ☐ Urgent | ☐ 24 hours | ☐ 20 working days |

Name of Company doing the work: 🏢

Name of person carrying out work: 🪪

| Work Start Date: | 📅 | Start Time: | am/pm |
|---|---|---|---|
| Work Finish Date: | 📅 | Finish Time: | am/pm |

| Is a return visit needed for this job? | ☐ YES ☐ NO |
|---|---|

# Return Visit Work

| Work Start Date: | 📅 | Start Time: | am/pm |
|---|---|---|---|
| Work Finish Date: | 📅 | Finish Time: | am/pm |

| Is a return visit needed for this job? | ☐ YES ☐ NO |
|---|---|

| Work Start Date: | 📅 | Start Time: | am/pm |
|---|---|---|---|
| Work Finish Date: | 📅 | Finish Time: | am/pm |

Date repair is completed:

Notes / Comments:

# Repairs Log Sheet

| Repair Job No: | Date: 📅 |
|---|---|

Name of person reporting repair: 👤

Where is the fault? 🔍

Description of fault / repair required:

| Priority given: | ☐ Emergency | ☐ Routine | ☐ 5 working days |
|---|---|---|---|
| | ☐ Urgent | ☐ 24 hours | ☐ 20 working days |

Name of Company doing the work: 🏢

Name of person carrying out work: 🪪

| Work Start Date: 📅 | Start Time: | am/pm |
|---|---|---|
| Work Finish Date: 📅 | Finish Time: | am/pm |

| Is a return visit needed for this job? | ☐ YES ☐ NO |
|---|---|

# Return Visit Work

| Work Start Date: 📅 | Start Time: | am/pm |
|---|---|---|
| Work Finish Date: 📅 | Finish Time: | am/pm |

| Is a return visit needed for this job? | ☐ YES ☐ NO |
|---|---|

| Work Start Date: 📅 | Start Time: | am/pm |
|---|---|---|
| Work Finish Date: 📅 | Finish Time: | am/pm |

Date repair is completed:

Notes / Comments:

# Repairs Log Sheet

| Repair Job No: | Date: |
|---|---|

Name of person reporting repair:

Where is the fault?

Description of fault / repair required:

| Priority given: | ☐ Emergency | ☐ Routine | ☐ 5 working days |
|---|---|---|---|
| | ☐ Urgent | ☐ 24 hours | ☐ 20 working days |

Name of Company doing the work:

Name of person carrying out work:

| Work Start Date: | Start Time: | am/pm |
|---|---|---|
| Work Finish Date: | Finish Time: | am/pm |

Is a return visit needed for this job?     ☐ YES  ☐ NO

# Return Visit Work

| Work Start Date: | Start Time: | am/pm |
|---|---|---|
| Work Finish Date: | Finish Time: | am/pm |

Is a return visit needed for this job?     ☐ YES  ☐ NO

| Work Start Date: | Start Time: | am/pm |
|---|---|---|
| Work Finish Date: | Finish Time: | am/pm |

Date repair is completed:

Notes / Comments:

# Repairs Log Sheet

| Repair Job No: | Date: |
|---|---|

Name of person reporting repair:

Where is the fault?

Description of fault / repair required:

| Priority given: | ☐ Emergency | ☐ Routine | ☐ 5 working days |
|---|---|---|---|
| | ☐ Urgent | ☐ 24 hours | ☐ 20 working days |

Name of Company doing the work:

Name of person carrying out work:

| Work Start Date: | Start Time: | am/pm |
|---|---|---|
| Work Finish Date: | Finish Time: | am/pm |

Is a return visit needed for this job?      ☐ YES  ☐ NO

# Return Visit Work

| Work Start Date: | Start Time: | am/pm |
|---|---|---|
| Work Finish Date: | Finish Time: | am/pm |

Is a return visit needed for this job?      ☐ YES  ☐ NO

| Work Start Date: | Start Time: | am/pm |
|---|---|---|
| Work Finish Date: | Finish Time: | am/pm |

Date repair is completed:

Notes / Comments:

# Repairs Log Sheet

| Repair Job No: | Date: 📅 |
|---|---|

Name of person reporting repair: 👤

Where is the fault? 🔍

Description of fault / repair required:

| Priority given: | ☐ Emergency | ☐ Routine | ☐ 5 working days |
|---|---|---|---|
| | ☐ Urgent | ☐ 24 hours | ☐ 20 working days |

Name of Company doing the work: 🏢

Name of person carrying out work: 🪪

| Work Start Date: 📅 | Start Time: am/pm |
|---|---|
| Work Finish Date: 📅 | Finish Time: am/pm |

Is a return visit needed for this job?   ☐ YES  ☐ NO

# Return Visit Work

| Work Start Date: 📅 | Start Time: am/pm |
|---|---|
| Work Finish Date: 📅 | Finish Time: am/pm |

Is a return visit needed for this job?   ☐ YES  ☐ NO

| Work Start Date: 📅 | Start Time: am/pm |
|---|---|
| Work Finish Date: 📅 | Finish Time: am/pm |

Date repair is completed:

Notes / Comments: _____

_____

_____

_____

_____

_____

# Repairs Log Sheet

| | |
|---|---|
| Repair Job No: | Date: 📅 |

Name of person reporting repair: 👤

Where is the fault? 🔍

Description of fault / repair required:

| Priority given: | ☐ Emergency | ☐ Routine | ☐ 5 working days |
|---|---|---|---|
| | ☐ Urgent | ☐ 24 hours | ☐ 20 working days |

Name of Company doing the work: 🏢

Name of person carrying out work: 🪪

| Work Start Date: 📅 | Start Time: | am/pm |
|---|---|---|
| Work Finish Date: 📅 | Finish Time: | am/pm |

| Is a return visit needed for this job? | ☐ YES ☐ NO |
|---|---|

# Return Visit Work

| Work Start Date: 📅 | Start Time: | am/pm |
|---|---|---|
| Work Finish Date: 📅 | Finish Time: | am/pm |

| Is a return visit needed for this job? | ☐ YES ☐ NO |
|---|---|

| Work Start Date: 📅 | Start Time: | am/pm |
|---|---|---|
| Work Finish Date: 📅 | Finish Time: | am/pm |

Date repair is completed:

Notes / Comments:

# Repairs Log Sheet

| | |
|---|---|
| Repair Job No: | Date: 📅 |

Name of person reporting repair: 👤

Where is the fault? 🔍

Description of fault / repair required:

| Priority given: | ☐ Emergency | ☐ Routine | ☐ 5 working days |
|---|---|---|---|
| | ☐ Urgent | ☐ 24 hours | ☐ 20 working days |

Name of Company doing the work: 🏢

Name of person carrying out work: 🪪

| Work Start Date: 📅 | Start Time: | am/pm |
|---|---|---|
| Work Finish Date: 📅 | Finish Time: | am/pm |

Is a return visit needed for this job?　　　　☐ YES ☐ NO

# Return Visit Work

| Work Start Date: 📅 | Start Time: | am/pm |
|---|---|---|
| Work Finish Date: 📅 | Finish Time: | am/pm |

Is a return visit needed for this job?　　　　☐ YES ☐ NO

| Work Start Date: 📅 | Start Time: | am/pm |
|---|---|---|
| Work Finish Date: 📅 | Finish Time: | am/pm |

Date repair is completed:

Notes / Comments:

# Repairs Log Sheet

| Repair Job No: | Date: | 📅 |
|---|---|---|

| Name of person reporting repair: | 👤 |
|---|---|

| Where is the fault? | 🔍 |
|---|---|

**Description of fault / repair required:**

| Priority given: | ☐ Emergency | ☐ Routine | ☐ 5 working days |
|---|---|---|---|
| | ☐ Urgent | ☐ 24 hours | ☐ 20 working days |

| Name of Company doing the work: | 🏢 |
|---|---|

| Name of person carrying out work: | 🪪 |
|---|---|

| Work Start Date: | 📅 | Start Time: | am/pm |
|---|---|---|---|
| Work Finish Date: | 📅 | Finish Time: | am/pm |

| Is a return visit needed for this job? | ☐ YES ☐ NO |
|---|---|

# Return Visit Work

| Work Start Date: | 📅 | Start Time: | am/pm |
|---|---|---|---|
| Work Finish Date: | 📅 | Finish Time: | am/pm |

| Is a return visit needed for this job? | ☐ YES ☐ NO |
|---|---|

| Work Start Date: | 📅 | Start Time: | am/pm |
|---|---|---|---|
| Work Finish Date: | 📅 | Finish Time: | am/pm |

Date repair is completed:

Notes / Comments:

# Repairs Log Sheet

Repair Job No: | Date:

Name of person reporting repair:

Where is the fault?

Description of fault / repair required:

Priority given:
- ☐ Emergency
- ☐ Urgent
- ☐ Routine
- ☐ 24 hours
- ☐ 5 working days
- ☐ 20 working days

Name of Company doing the work:

Name of person carrying out work:

Work Start Date: | Start Time: | am/pm

Work Finish Date: | Finish Time: | am/pm

Is a return visit needed for this job? ☐ YES ☐ NO

# Return Visit Work

Work Start Date: | Start Time: | am/pm

Work Finish Date: | Finish Time: | am/pm

Is a return visit needed for this job? ☐ YES ☐ NO

Work Start Date: | Start Time: | am/pm

Work Finish Date: | Finish Time: | am/pm

Date repair is completed:

Notes / Comments:

# Repairs Log Sheet

| Repair Job No: | Date: | 📅 |
|---|---|---|

Name of person reporting repair: 👤

Where is the fault? 🔍

Description of fault / repair required:

| Priority given: | ☐ Emergency | ☐ Routine | ☐ 5 working days |
|---|---|---|---|
| | ☐ Urgent | ☐ 24 hours | ☐ 20 working days |

Name of Company doing the work: 🏢

Name of person carrying out work: 🪪

| Work Start Date: | 📅 | Start Time: | am/pm |
|---|---|---|---|
| Work Finish Date: | 📅 | Finish Time: | am/pm |

Is a return visit needed for this job?   ☐ YES ☐ NO

# Return Visit Work

| Work Start Date: | 📅 | Start Time: | am/pm |
|---|---|---|---|
| Work Finish Date: | 📅 | Finish Time: | am/pm |

Is a return visit needed for this job?   ☐ YES ☐ NO

| Work Start Date: | 📅 | Start Time: | am/pm |
|---|---|---|---|
| Work Finish Date: | 📅 | Finish Time: | am/pm |

Date repair is completed:

Notes / Comments:

# Repairs Log Sheet

| Repair Job No: | Date: 📅 |
| --- | --- |

Name of person reporting repair: 👤

Where is the fault? 🔍

Description of fault / repair required:

| Priority given: | ☐ Emergency | ☐ Routine | ☐ 5 working days |
| --- | --- | --- | --- |
| | ☐ Urgent | ☐ 24 hours | ☐ 20 working days |

Name of Company doing the work: 🏢

Name of person carrying out work: 🪪

| Work Start Date: 📅 | Start Time: am/pm |
| --- | --- |
| Work Finish Date: 📅 | Finish Time: am/pm |

| Is a return visit needed for this job? | ☐ YES ☐ NO |
| --- | --- |

# Return Visit Work

| Work Start Date: 📅 | Start Time: am/pm |
| --- | --- |
| Work Finish Date: 📅 | Finish Time: am/pm |

| Is a return visit needed for this job? | ☐ YES ☐ NO |
| --- | --- |

| Work Start Date: 📅 | Start Time: am/pm |
| --- | --- |
| Work Finish Date: 📅 | Finish Time: am/pm |

Date repair is completed:

Notes / Comments:

# Repairs Log Sheet

| Repair Job No: | Date: | 📅 |
|---|---|---|

| Name of person reporting repair: | 👤 |
|---|---|

| Where is the fault? | 🔍 |
|---|---|

Description of fault / repair required:

| Priority given: | ☐ Emergency | ☐ Routine | ☐ 5 working days |
|---|---|---|---|
| | ☐ Urgent | ☐ 24 hours | ☐ 20 working days |

| Name of Company doing the work: | 🏢 |
|---|---|

| Name of person carrying out work: | 🆔 |
|---|---|

| Work Start Date: | 📅 | Start Time: | am/pm |
|---|---|---|---|
| Work Finish Date: | 📅 | Finish Time: | am/pm |

| Is a return visit needed for this job? | ☐ YES ☐ NO |
|---|---|

# Return Visit Work

| Work Start Date: | 📅 | Start Time: | am/pm |
|---|---|---|---|
| Work Finish Date: | 📅 | Finish Time: | am/pm |
| Is a return visit needed for this job? | | ☐ YES ☐ NO | |
| Work Start Date: | 📅 | Start Time: | am/pm |
| Work Finish Date: | 📅 | Finish Time: | am/pm |

Date repair is completed:

Notes / Comments:

_____

_____

_____

_____

_____

# Repairs Log Sheet

| Repair Job No: | Date: | 📅 |
|---|---|---|

Name of person reporting repair: 👤

Where is the fault? 🔍

Description of fault / repair required:

| Priority given: | ☐ Emergency | ☐ Routine | ☐ 5 working days |
|---|---|---|---|
| | ☐ Urgent | ☐ 24 hours | ☐ 20 working days |

Name of Company doing the work: 🏢

Name of person carrying out work: 🪪

| Work Start Date: | 📅 | Start Time: | am/pm |
|---|---|---|---|
| Work Finish Date: | 📅 | Finish Time: | am/pm |

Is a return visit needed for this job?  ☐ YES  ☐ NO

# Return Visit Work

| Work Start Date: | 📅 | Start Time: | am/pm |
|---|---|---|---|
| Work Finish Date: | 📅 | Finish Time: | am/pm |

Is a return visit needed for this job?  ☐ YES  ☐ NO

| Work Start Date: | 📅 | Start Time: | am/pm |
|---|---|---|---|
| Work Finish Date: | 📅 | Finish Time: | am/pm |

Date repair is completed:

Notes / Comments:

# Repairs Log Sheet

| | |
|---|---|
| Repair Job No: | Date: |

Name of person reporting repair:

Where is the fault?

Description of fault / repair required:

| Priority given: | ☐ Emergency | ☐ Routine | ☐ 5 working days |
|---|---|---|---|
| | ☐ Urgent | ☐ 24 hours | ☐ 20 working days |

Name of Company doing the work:

Name of person carrying out work:

| | | | |
|---|---|---|---|
| Work Start Date: | | Start Time: | am/pm |
| Work Finish Date: | | Finish Time: | am/pm |
| Is a return visit needed for this job? | ☐ YES ☐ NO | | |

# Return Visit Work

| | | | |
|---|---|---|---|
| Work Start Date: | | Start Time: | am/pm |
| Work Finish Date: | | Finish Time: | am/pm |
| Is a return visit needed for this job? | ☐ YES ☐ NO | | |
| Work Start Date: | | Start Time: | am/pm |
| Work Finish Date: | | Finish Time: | am/pm |
| Date repair is completed: | | | |

Notes / Comments:

# Repairs Log Sheet

| Repair Job No: | Date: | |

Name of person reporting repair:

Where is the fault?

Description of fault / repair required:

| Priority given: | ☐ Emergency | ☐ Routine | ☐ 5 working days |
| | ☐ Urgent | ☐ 24 hours | ☐ 20 working days |

Name of Company doing the work:

Name of person carrying out work:

| Work Start Date: | Start Time: | am/pm |
| Work Finish Date: | Finish Time: | am/pm |
| Is a return visit needed for this job? | ☐ YES ☐ NO | |

# Return Visit Work

| Work Start Date: | Start Time: | am/pm |
| Work Finish Date: | Finish Time: | am/pm |
| Is a return visit needed for this job? | ☐ YES ☐ NO | |
| Work Start Date: | Start Time: | am/pm |
| Work Finish Date: | Finish Time: | am/pm |

Date repair is completed:

Notes / Comments:

# Repairs Log Sheet

| Repair Job No: | Date: | 📅 |
|---|---|---|

**Name of person reporting repair:** 👤

**Where is the fault?** 🔍

**Description of fault / repair required:**

| Priority given: | ☐ Emergency | ☐ Routine | ☐ 5 working days |
|---|---|---|---|
| | ☐ Urgent | ☐ 24 hours | ☐ 20 working days |

**Name of Company doing the work:** 🏢

**Name of person carrying out work:** 🪪

| Work Start Date: | 📅 | Start Time: | am/pm |
|---|---|---|---|
| Work Finish Date: | 📅 | Finish Time: | am/pm |

Is a return visit needed for this job?          ☐ YES   ☐ NO

# Return Visit Work

| Work Start Date: | 📅 | Start Time: | am/pm |
|---|---|---|---|
| Work Finish Date: | 📅 | Finish Time: | am/pm |

Is a return visit needed for this job?          ☐ YES   ☐ NO

| Work Start Date: | 📅 | Start Time: | am/pm |
|---|---|---|---|
| Work Finish Date: | 📅 | Finish Time: | am/pm |

Date repair is completed:

Notes / Comments:

# Repairs Log Sheet

| Repair Job No: | Date: | 📅 |
|---|---|---|

| Name of person reporting repair: | 👤 |
|---|---|

| Where is the fault? | 🔍 |
|---|---|

**Description of fault / repair required:**

| Priority given: | ☐ Emergency | ☐ Routine | ☐ 5 working days |
|---|---|---|---|
| | ☐ Urgent | ☐ 24 hours | ☐ 20 working days |

| Name of Company doing the work: | 🏢 |
|---|---|

| Name of person carrying out work: | 🪪 ID |
|---|---|

| Work Start Date: | 📅 | Start Time: | am/pm |
|---|---|---|---|
| Work Finish Date: | 📅 | Finish Time: | am/pm |

| Is a return visit needed for this job? | ☐ YES ☐ NO |
|---|---|

# Return Visit Work

| Work Start Date: | 📅 | Start Time: | am/pm |
|---|---|---|---|
| Work Finish Date: | 📅 | Finish Time: | am/pm |

| Is a return visit needed for this job? | ☐ YES ☐ NO |
|---|---|

| Work Start Date: | 📅 | Start Time: | am/pm |
|---|---|---|---|
| Work Finish Date: | 📅 | Finish Time: | am/pm |

| Date repair is completed: |
|---|

**Notes / Comments:**

# Repairs Log Sheet

| Repair Job No: | Date: | 📅 |

Name of person reporting repair: 👤

Where is the fault? 🔍

Description of fault / repair required:

| Priority given: | ☐ Emergency | ☐ Routine | ☐ 5 working days |
| | ☐ Urgent | ☐ 24 hours | ☐ 20 working days |

Name of Company doing the work: 🏢

Name of person carrying out work: 🪪

| Work Start Date: | 📅 | Start Time: | am/pm |
| Work Finish Date: | 📅 | Finish Time: | am/pm |

Is a return visit needed for this job?   ☐ YES ☐ NO

# Return Visit Work

| Work Start Date: | 📅 | Start Time: | am/pm |
| Work Finish Date: | 📅 | Finish Time: | am/pm |

Is a return visit needed for this job?   ☐ YES ☐ NO

| Work Start Date: | 📅 | Start Time: | am/pm |
| Work Finish Date: | 📅 | Finish Time: | am/pm |

Date repair is completed:

Notes / Comments:

# Repairs Log Sheet

| | |
|---|---|
| Repair Job No: | Date: |

Name of person reporting repair:

Where is the fault?

Description of fault / repair required:

| Priority given: | ☐ Emergency | ☐ Routine | ☐ 5 working days |
|---|---|---|---|
| | ☐ Urgent | ☐ 24 hours | ☐ 20 working days |

Name of Company doing the work:

Name of person carrying out work:

| | | |
|---|---|---|
| Work Start Date: | Start Time: | am/pm |
| Work Finish Date: | Finish Time: | am/pm |
| Is a return visit needed for this job? | ☐ YES ☐ NO | |

# Return Visit Work

| | | |
|---|---|---|
| Work Start Date: | Start Time: | am/pm |
| Work Finish Date: | Finish Time: | am/pm |
| Is a return visit needed for this job? | ☐ YES ☐ NO | |
| Work Start Date: | Start Time: | am/pm |
| Work Finish Date: | Finish Time: | am/pm |
| Date repair is completed: | | |

Notes / Comments:

# Repairs Log Sheet

| | |
|---|---|
| Repair Job No: | Date: |

Name of person reporting repair:

Where is the fault?

Description of fault / repair required:

| Priority given: | ☐ Emergency | ☐ Routine | ☐ 5 working days |
|---|---|---|---|
| | ☐ Urgent | ☐ 24 hours | ☐ 20 working days |

Name of Company doing the work:

Name of person carrying out work:

| Work Start Date: | Start Time: | am/pm |
|---|---|---|
| Work Finish Date: | Finish Time: | am/pm |

| Is a return visit needed for this job? | ☐ YES ☐ NO |
|---|---|

# Return Visit Work

| Work Start Date: | Start Time: | am/pm |
|---|---|---|
| Work Finish Date: | Finish Time: | am/pm |

| Is a return visit needed for this job? | ☐ YES ☐ NO |
|---|---|

| Work Start Date: | Start Time: | am/pm |
|---|---|---|
| Work Finish Date: | Finish Time: | am/pm |

Date repair is completed:

Notes / Comments:

# Repairs Log Sheet

| Repair Job No: | Date: | 📅 |
|---|---|---|

Name of person reporting repair: 👤

Where is the fault? 🔍

Description of fault / repair required:

Priority given:
- ☐ Emergency
- ☐ Urgent
- ☐ Routine
- ☐ 24 hours
- ☐ 5 working days
- ☐ 20 working days

Name of Company doing the work: 🏢

Name of person carrying out work: 🆔

| Work Start Date: | 📅 | Start Time: | am/pm |
|---|---|---|---|
| Work Finish Date: | 📅 | Finish Time: | am/pm |

Is a return visit needed for this job?     ☐ YES  ☐ NO

# Return Visit Work

| Work Start Date: | 📅 | Start Time: | am/pm |
|---|---|---|---|
| Work Finish Date: | 📅 | Finish Time: | am/pm |

Is a return visit needed for this job?     ☐ YES  ☐ NO

| Work Start Date: | 📅 | Start Time: | am/pm |
|---|---|---|---|
| Work Finish Date: | 📅 | Finish Time: | am/pm |

Date repair is completed:

Notes / Comments:

# Repairs Log Sheet

| Repair Job No: | Date: | 📅 |
|---|---|---|

| Name of person reporting repair: | 👤 |
|---|---|

| Where is the fault? | 🔍 |
|---|---|

Description of fault / repair required:

| Priority given: | ☐ Emergency | ☐ Routine | ☐ 5 working days |
|---|---|---|---|
| | ☐ Urgent | ☐ 24 hours | ☐ 20 working days |

| Name of Company doing the work: | 🏢 |
|---|---|

| Name of person carrying out work: | 🆔 |
|---|---|

| Work Start Date: | 📅 | Start Time: | am/pm |
|---|---|---|---|
| Work Finish Date: | 📅 | Finish Time: | am/pm |

| Is a return visit needed for this job? | ☐ YES ☐ NO |
|---|---|

# Return Visit Work

| Work Start Date: | 📅 | Start Time: | am/pm |
|---|---|---|---|
| Work Finish Date: | 📅 | Finish Time: | am/pm |
| Is a return visit needed for this job? | | ☐ YES ☐ NO | |
| Work Start Date: | 📅 | Start Time: | am/pm |
| Work Finish Date: | 📅 | Finish Time: | am/pm |

Date repair is completed:

Notes / Comments:

# Repairs Log Sheet

| Repair Job No: | Date: | 📅 |
|---|---|---|

Name of person reporting repair: 👤

Where is the fault? 🔍

Description of fault / repair required:

Priority given:
- ☐ Emergency ☐ Routine ☐ 5 working days
- ☐ Urgent ☐ 24 hours ☐ 20 working days

Name of Company doing the work: 🏢

Name of person carrying out work: 🪪

| Work Start Date: | 📅 | Start Time: | am/pm |
|---|---|---|---|
| Work Finish Date: | 📅 | Finish Time: | am/pm |

Is a return visit needed for this job? ☐ YES ☐ NO

# Return Visit Work

| Work Start Date: | 📅 | Start Time: | am/pm |
|---|---|---|---|
| Work Finish Date: | 📅 | Finish Time: | am/pm |

Is a return visit needed for this job? ☐ YES ☐ NO

| Work Start Date: | 📅 | Start Time: | am/pm |
|---|---|---|---|
| Work Finish Date: | 📅 | Finish Time: | am/pm |

Date repair is completed:

Notes / Comments:

# Repairs Log Sheet

| | |
|---|---|
| Ropair Job No: | Date: 📅 |

Name of person reporting repair: 👤

Where is the fault? 🔍

Description of fault / repair required:

| Priority given: | ☐ Emergency | ☐ Routine | ☐ 5 working days |
|---|---|---|---|
| | ☐ Urgent | ☐ 24 hours | ☐ 20 working days |

Name of Company doing the work: 🏢

Name of person carrying out work: 🪪

| Work Start Date: | 📅 | Start Time: | am/pm |
|---|---|---|---|
| Work Finish Date: | 📅 | Finish Time: | am/pm |

| Is a return visit needed for this job? | ☐ YES ☐ NO |
|---|---|

# Return Visit Work

| Work Start Date: | 📅 | Start Time: | am/pm |
|---|---|---|---|
| Work Finish Date: | 📅 | Finish Time: | am/pm |

| Is a return visit needed for this job? | ☐ YES ☐ NO |
|---|---|

| Work Start Date: | 📅 | Start Time: | am/pm |
|---|---|---|---|
| Work Finish Date: | 📅 | Finish Time: | am/pm |

Date repair is completed:

Notes / Comments:

# Repairs Log Sheet

| Repair Job No: | Date: |
|---|---|

Name of person reporting repair:

Where is the fault?

Description of fault / repair required:

Priority given:
- ☐ Emergency
- ☐ Urgent
- ☐ Routine
- ☐ 24 hours
- ☐ 5 working days
- ☐ 20 working days

Name of Company doing the work:

Name of person carrying out work:

| Work Start Date: | Start Time: | am/pm |
|---|---|---|
| Work Finish Date: | Finish Time: | am/pm |

Is a return visit needed for this job?  ☐ YES  ☐ NO

# Return Visit Work

| Work Start Date: | Start Time: | am/pm |
|---|---|---|
| Work Finish Date: | Finish Time: | am/pm |

Is a return visit needed for this job?  ☐ YES  ☐ NO

| Work Start Date: | Start Time: | am/pm |
|---|---|---|
| Work Finish Date: | Finish Time: | am/pm |

Date repair is completed:

Notes / Comments:

# Repairs Log Sheet

| Repair Job No: | Date: | 📅 |
|---|---|---|

Name of person reporting repair: 👤

Where is the fault? 🔍

Description of fault / repair required:

| Priority given: | ☐ Emergency | ☐ Routine | ☐ 5 working days |
|---|---|---|---|
| | ☐ Urgent | ☐ 24 hours | ☐ 20 working days |

Name of Company doing the work: 🏢

Name of person carrying out work: 🆔

| Work Start Date: | 📅 | Start Time: | am/pm |
|---|---|---|---|
| Work Finish Date: | 📅 | Finish Time: | am/pm |

Is a return visit needed for this job?          ☐ YES  ☐ NO

# Return Visit Work

| Work Start Date: | 📅 | Start Time: | am/pm |
|---|---|---|---|
| Work Finish Date: | 📅 | Finish Time: | am/pm |

Is a return visit needed for this job?          ☐ YES  ☐ NO

| Work Start Date: | 📅 | Start Time: | am/pm |
|---|---|---|---|
| Work Finish Date: | 📅 | Finish Time: | am/pm |

Date repair is completed:

Notes / Comments:

# Repairs Log Sheet

| Repair Job No: | Date: |
|---|---|

Name of person reporting repair:

Where is the fault?

Description of fault / repair required:

| Priority given: | ☐ Emergency | ☐ Routine | ☐ 5 working days |
|---|---|---|---|
| | ☐ Urgent | ☐ 24 hours | ☐ 20 working days |

Name of Company doing the work:

Name of person carrying out work:

| Work Start Date: | | Start Time: | am/pm |
|---|---|---|---|
| Work Finish Date: | | Finish Time: | am/pm |

| Is a return visit needed for this job? | ☐ YES ☐ NO |
|---|---|

# Return Visit Work

| Work Start Date: | | Start Time: | am/pm |
|---|---|---|---|
| Work Finish Date: | | Finish Time: | am/pm |

| Is a return visit needed for this job? | ☐ YES ☐ NO |
|---|---|

| Work Start Date: | | Start Time: | am/pm |
|---|---|---|---|
| Work Finish Date: | | Finish Time: | am/pm |

Date repair is completed:

Notes / Comments:

# Repairs Log Sheet

| Repair Job No: | Date: | 📅 |
| --- | --- | --- |

Name of person reporting repair: 👤

Where is the fault? 🔍

Description of fault / repair required:

| Priority given: | ☐ Emergency | ☐ Routine | ☐ 5 working days |
| --- | --- | --- | --- |
| | ☐ Urgent | ☐ 24 hours | ☐ 20 working days |

Name of Company doing the work: 🏢

Name of person carrying out work: 🆔

| Work Start Date: | 📅 | Start Time: | am/pm |
| --- | --- | --- | --- |
| Work Finish Date: | 📅 | Finish Time: | am/pm |
| Is a return visit needed for this job? | | ☐ YES ☐ NO | |

# Return Visit Work

| Work Start Date: | 📅 | Start Time: | am/pm |
| --- | --- | --- | --- |
| Work Finish Date: | 📅 | Finish Time: | am/pm |
| Is a return visit needed for this job? | | ☐ YES ☐ NO | |
| Work Start Date: | 📅 | Start Time: | am/pm |
| Work Finish Date: | 📅 | Finish Time: | am/pm |
| Date repair is completed: | | | |

Notes / Comments:

# Repairs Log Sheet

| Repair Job No: | Date: | 📅 |
|---|---|---|

Name of person reporting repair: 👤

Where is the fault? 🔍

Description of fault / repair required:

| Priority given: | ☐ Emergency | ☐ Routine | ☐ 5 working days |
|---|---|---|---|
| | ☐ Urgent | ☐ 24 hours | ☐ 20 working days |

Name of Company doing the work: 🏢

Name of person carrying out work: 🪪

| Work Start Date: | 📅 | Start Time: | am/pm |
|---|---|---|---|
| Work Finish Date: | 📅 | Finish Time: | am/pm |

Is a return visit needed for this job?  ☐ YES  ☐ NO

# Return Visit Work

| Work Start Date: | 📅 | Start Time: | am/pm |
|---|---|---|---|
| Work Finish Date: | 📅 | Finish Time: | am/pm |

Is a return visit needed for this job?  ☐ YES  ☐ NO

| Work Start Date: | 📅 | Start Time: | am/pm |
|---|---|---|---|
| Work Finish Date: | 📅 | Finish Time: | am/pm |

Date repair is completed:

Notes / Comments:

# Repairs Log Sheet

| | |
|---|---|
| Repair Job No: | Date: 📅 |

Name of person reporting repair: 👤

Where is the fault? 🔍

Description of fault / repair required:

| Priority given: | ☐ Emergency | ☐ Routine | ☐ 5 working days |
|---|---|---|---|
| | ☐ Urgent | ☐ 24 hours | ☐ 20 working days |

Name of Company doing the work: 🏢

Name of person carrying out work: 🪪

| Work Start Date: 📅 | Start Time: | am/pm |
|---|---|---|
| Work Finish Date: 📅 | Finish Time: | am/pm |

| Is a return visit needed for this job? | ☐ YES ☐ NO |
|---|---|

# Return Visit Work

| Work Start Date: 📅 | Start Time: | am/pm |
|---|---|---|
| Work Finish Date: 📅 | Finish Time: | am/pm |

| Is a return visit needed for this job? | ☐ YES ☐ NO |
|---|---|

| Work Start Date: 📅 | Start Time: | am/pm |
|---|---|---|
| Work Finish Date: 📅 | Finish Time: | am/pm |

Date repair is completed:

Notes / Comments: _____
_____
_____
_____
_____

# Repairs Log Sheet

| Repair Job No: | Date: |
|---|---|

Name of person reporting repair:

Where is the fault?

Description of fault / repair required:

| Priority given: | ☐ Emergency | ☐ Routine | ☐ 5 working days |
|---|---|---|---|
| | ☐ Urgent | ☐ 24 hours | ☐ 20 working days |

Name of Company doing the work:

Name of person carrying out work:

| Work Start Date: | | Start Time: | am/pm |
|---|---|---|---|
| Work Finish Date: | | Finish Time: | am/pm |

| Is a return visit needed for this job? | ☐ YES ☐ NO |
|---|---|

# Return Visit Work

| Work Start Date: | | Start Time: | am/pm |
|---|---|---|---|
| Work Finish Date: | | Finish Time: | am/pm |
| Is a return visit needed for this job? | | ☐ YES ☐ NO | |
| Work Start Date: | | Start Time: | am/pm |
| Work Finish Date: | | Finish Time: | am/pm |

Date repair is completed:

Notes / Comments:

# Repairs Log Sheet

| Repair Job No: | Date: | 📅 |

Name of person reporting repair: 👤

Where is the fault? 🔍

Description of fault / repair required:

| Priority given: | ☐ Emergency | ☐ Routine | ☐ 5 working days |
| | ☐ Urgent | ☐ 24 hours | ☐ 20 working days |

Name of Company doing the work: 🏢

Name of person carrying out work: 🪪

| Work Start Date: | 📅 | Start Time: | am/pm |
| Work Finish Date: | 📅 | Finish Time: | am/pm |

Is a return visit needed for this job?　　　☐ YES ☐ NO

# Return Visit Work

| Work Start Date: | 📅 | Start Time: | am/pm |
| Work Finish Date: | 📅 | Finish Time: | am/pm |

Is a return visit needed for this job?　　　☐ YES ☐ NO

| Work Start Date: | 📅 | Start Time: | am/pm |
| Work Finish Date: | 📅 | Finish Time: | am/pm |

Date repair is completed:

Notes / Comments: _____

_____

_____

_____

_____

_____

# Repairs Log Sheet

| Repair Job No: | Date: |
|---|---|

Name of person reporting repair:

Where is the fault?

Description of fault / repair required:

| Priority given: | ☐ Emergency | ☐ Routine | ☐ 5 working days |
|---|---|---|---|
| | ☐ Urgent | ☐ 24 hours | ☐ 20 working days |

Name of Company doing the work:

Name of person carrying out work:

| Work Start Date: | Start Time: | am/pm |
|---|---|---|
| Work Finish Date: | Finish Time: | am/pm |

| Is a return visit needed for this job? | ☐ YES ☐ NO |
|---|---|

# Return Visit Work

| Work Start Date: | Start Time: | am/pm |
|---|---|---|
| Work Finish Date: | Finish Time: | am/pm |

| Is a return visit needed for this job? | ☐ YES ☐ NO |
|---|---|

| Work Start Date: | Start Time: | am/pm |
|---|---|---|
| Work Finish Date: | Finish Time: | am/pm |

Date repair is completed:

Notes / Comments:

# Repairs Log Sheet

| | | |
|---|---|---|
| **Repair Job No:** | **Date:** | 📅 |

**Name of person reporting repair:**

**Where is the fault?** 🔍

**Description of fault / repair required:**

**Priority given:**

| | | | | |
|---|---|---|---|---|
| ☐ Emergency | ☐ Routine | ☐ 5 working days |
| ☐ Urgent | ☐ 24 hours | ☐ 20 working days |

**Name of Company doing the work:** 🏢

**Name of person carrying out work:** 🪪

| | | |
|---|---|---|
| **Work Start Date:** | 📅 **Start Time:** | am/pm |
| **Work Finish Date:** | 📅 **Finish Time:** | am/pm |
| **Is a return visit needed for this job?** | ☐ YES ☐ NO | |

# Return Visit Work

| | | |
|---|---|---|
| **Work Start Date:** | 📅 **Start Time:** | am/pm |
| **Work Finish Date:** | 📅 **Finish Time:** | am/pm |
| **Is a return visit needed for this job?** | ☐ YES ☐ NO | |
| **Work Start Date:** | 📅 **Start Time:** | am/pm |
| **Work Finish Date:** | 📅 **Finish Time:** | am/pm |
| **Date repair is completed:** | | |

**Notes / Comments:**

# Repairs Log Sheet

| | |
|---|---|
| Repair Job No: | Date: |

Name of person reporting repair:

Where is the fault?

Description of fault / repair required:

Priority given:
- ☐ Emergency  ☐ Routine  ☐ 5 working days
- ☐ Urgent  ☐ 24 hours  ☐ 20 working days

Name of Company doing the work:

Name of person carrying out work:

| | | |
|---|---|---|
| Work Start Date: | Start Time: | am/pm |
| Work Finish Date: | Finish Time: | am/pm |

Is a return visit needed for this job?  ☐ YES  ☐ NO

# Return Visit Work

| | | |
|---|---|---|
| Work Start Date: | Start Time: | am/pm |
| Work Finish Date: | Finish Time: | am/pm |

Is a return visit needed for this job?  ☐ YES  ☐ NO

| | | |
|---|---|---|
| Work Start Date: | Start Time: | am/pm |
| Work Finish Date: | Finish Time: | am/pm |

Date repair is completed:

Notes / Comments:

# Repairs Log Sheet

| Repair Job No: | Date: 📅 |
|---|---|

**Name of person reporting repair:** 👤

**Where is the fault?** 🔍

**Description of fault / repair required:**

| Priority given: | ☐ Emergency | ☐ Routine | ☐ 5 working days |
|---|---|---|---|
| | ☐ Urgent | ☐ 24 hours | ☐ 20 working days |

**Name of Company doing the work:** 🏢

**Name of person carrying out work:** 🪪

| Work Start Date: 📅 | Start Time: am/pm |
|---|---|
| Work Finish Date: 📅 | Finish Time: am/pm |

| Is a return visit needed for this job? | ☐ YES ☐ NO |
|---|---|

# Return Visit Work

| Work Start Date: 📅 | Start Time: am/pm |
|---|---|
| Work Finish Date: 📅 | Finish Time: am/pm |

| Is a return visit needed for this job? | ☐ YES ☐ NO |
|---|---|

| Work Start Date: 📅 | Start Time: am/pm |
|---|---|
| Work Finish Date: 📅 | Finish Time: am/pm |

**Date repair is completed:**

**Notes / Comments:**

# Repairs Log Sheet

| Repair Job No: | Date: |
|---|---|

Name of person reporting repair:

Where is the fault?

Description of fault / repair required:

| Priority given: | ☐ Emergency | ☐ Routine | ☐ 5 working days |
|---|---|---|---|
| | ☐ Urgent | ☐ 24 hours | ☐ 20 working days |

Name of Company doing the work:

Name of person carrying out work:

| Work Start Date: | Start Time: | am/pm |
|---|---|---|
| Work Finish Date: | Finish Time: | am/pm |

| Is a return visit needed for this job? | ☐ YES ☐ NO |
|---|---|

# Return Visit Work

| Work Start Date: | Start Time: | am/pm |
|---|---|---|
| Work Finish Date: | Finish Time: | am/pm |

| Is a return visit needed for this job? | ☐ YES ☐ NO |
|---|---|

| Work Start Date: | Start Time: | am/pm |
|---|---|---|
| Work Finish Date: | Finish Time: | am/pm |

Date repair is completed:

Notes / Comments:

# Repairs Log Sheet

| Repair Job No: | Date: | 📅 |
|---|---|---|

| Name of person reporting repair: | 👤 |
|---|---|

| Where is the fault? | 🔍 |
|---|---|

| Description of fault / repair required: |
|---|

| Priority given: | ☐ Emergency ☐ Urgent | ☐ Routine ☐ 24 hours | ☐ 5 working days ☐ 20 working days |
|---|---|---|---|

| Name of Company doing the work: | 🏢 |
|---|---|

| Name of person carrying out work: | 🪪 ID |
|---|---|

| Work Start Date: | 📅 | Start Time: | am/pm |
|---|---|---|---|
| Work Finish Date: | 📅 | Finish Time: | am/pm |

| Is a return visit needed for this job? | ☐ YES ☐ NO |
|---|---|

# Return Visit Work

| Work Start Date: | 📅 | Start Time: | am/pm |
|---|---|---|---|
| Work Finish Date: | 📅 | Finish Time: | am/pm |
| Is a return visit needed for this job? | | ☐ YES ☐ NO | |
| Work Start Date: | 📅 | Start Time: | am/pm |
| Work Finish Date: | 📅 | Finish Time: | am/pm |
| Date repair is completed: | | | |

Notes / Comments:

# Repairs Log Sheet

| Repair Job No: | Date: |
|---|---|

Name of person reporting repair:

Where is the fault?

Description of fault / repair required:

| Priority given: | ☐ Emergency | ☐ Routine | ☐ 5 working days |
|---|---|---|---|
| | ☐ Urgent | ☐ 24 hours | ☐ 20 working days |

Name of Company doing the work:

Name of person carrying out work:

| Work Start Date: | Start Time: | am/pm |
|---|---|---|
| Work Finish Date: | Finish Time: | am/pm |

Is a return visit needed for this job?     ☐ YES  ☐ NO

# Return Visit Work

| Work Start Date: | Start Time: | am/pm |
|---|---|---|
| Work Finish Date: | Finish Time: | am/pm |

Is a return visit needed for this job?     ☐ YES  ☐ NO

| Work Start Date: | Start Time: | am/pm |
|---|---|---|
| Work Finish Date: | Finish Time: | am/pm |

Date repair is completed:

Notes / Comments:

# Repairs Log Sheet

| Repair Job No: | Date: | 📅 |
|---|---|---|

| Name of person reporting repair: | 👤 |
|---|---|

| Where is the fault? | 🔍 |
|---|---|

Description of fault / repair required:

| Priority given: | ☐ Emergency | ☐ Routine | ☐ 5 working days |
|---|---|---|---|
| | ☐ Urgent | ☐ 24 hours | ☐ 20 working days |

| Name of Company doing the work: | 🏢 |
|---|---|

| Name of person carrying out work: | 🆔 |
|---|---|

| Work Start Date: | 📅 | Start Time: | am/pm |
|---|---|---|---|
| Work Finish Date: | 📅 | Finish Time: | am/pm |

| Is a return visit needed for this job? | ☐ YES ☐ NO |
|---|---|

# Return Visit Work

| Work Start Date: | 📅 | Start Time: | am/pm |
|---|---|---|---|
| Work Finish Date: | 📅 | Finish Time: | am/pm |
| Is a return visit needed for this job? | | ☐ YES ☐ NO | |
| Work Start Date: | 📅 | Start Time: | am/pm |
| Work Finish Date: | 📅 | Finish Time: | am/pm |

Date repair is completed:

Notes / Comments:

# Repairs Log Sheet

| Repair Job No: | Date: |
|---|---|

Name of person reporting repair:

Where is the fault?

Description of fault / repair required:

Priority given:
- ☐ Emergency   ☐ Routine   ☐ 5 working days
- ☐ Urgent   ☐ 24 hours   ☐ 20 working days

Name of Company doing the work:

Name of person carrying out work:

| Work Start Date: | Start Time: | am/pm |
|---|---|---|
| Work Finish Date: | Finish Time: | am/pm |

Is a return visit needed for this job?   ☐ YES   ☐ NO

# Return Visit Work

| Work Start Date: | Start Time: | am/pm |
|---|---|---|
| Work Finish Date: | Finish Time: | am/pm |

Is a return visit needed for this job?   ☐ YES   ☐ NO

| Work Start Date: | Start Time: | am/pm |
|---|---|---|
| Work Finish Date: | Finish Time: | am/pm |

Date repair is completed:

Notes / Comments:

# Repairs Log Sheet

| | |
|---|---|
| Repair Job No: | Date: |

Name of person reporting repair:

Where is the fault?

Description of fault / repair required:

| Priority given: | ☐ Emergency | ☐ Routine | ☐ 5 working days |
|---|---|---|---|
| | ☐ Urgent | ☐ 24 hours | ☐ 20 working days |

Name of Company doing the work:

Name of person carrying out work:

| Work Start Date: | Start Time: | am/pm |
|---|---|---|
| Work Finish Date: | Finish Time: | am/pm |

| Is a return visit needed for this job? | ☐ YES ☐ NO |
|---|---|

# Return Visit Work

| Work Start Date: | Start Time: | am/pm |
|---|---|---|
| Work Finish Date: | Finish Time: | am/pm |

| Is a return visit needed for this job? | ☐ YES ☐ NO |
|---|---|

| Work Start Date: | Start Time: | am/pm |
|---|---|---|
| Work Finish Date: | Finish Time: | am/pm |

Date repair is completed:

Notes / Comments:

# Repairs Log Sheet

| Repair Job No: | Date: 📅 |
|---|---|

Name of person reporting repair: 👤

Where is the fault? 🔍

Description of fault / repair required:

| Priority given: | ☐ Emergency | ☐ Routine | ☐ 5 working days |
|---|---|---|---|
| | ☐ Urgent | ☐ 24 hours | ☐ 20 working days |

Name of Company doing the work: 🏢

Name of person carrying out work: 🆔

| Work Start Date: 📅 | Start Time: | am/pm |
|---|---|---|
| Work Finish Date: 📅 | Finish Time: | am/pm |

| Is a return visit needed for this job? | ☐ YES ☐ NO |
|---|---|

# Return Visit Work

| Work Start Date: 📅 | Start Time: | am/pm |
|---|---|---|
| Work Finish Date: 📅 | Finish Time: | am/pm |

| Is a return visit needed for this job? | ☐ YES ☐ NO |
|---|---|

| Work Start Date: 📅 | Start Time: | am/pm |
|---|---|---|
| Work Finish Date: 📅 | Finish Time: | am/pm |

Date repair is completed:

Notes / Comments:

# Repairs Log Sheet

| | |
|---|---|
| Repair Job No: | Date: |

Name of person reporting repair:

Where is the fault?

Description of fault / repair required:

Priority given:
- ☐ Emergency
- ☐ Urgent
- ☐ Routine
- ☐ 24 hours
- ☐ 5 working days
- ☐ 20 working days

Name of Company doing the work:

Name of person carrying out work:

| | | |
|---|---|---|
| Work Start Date: | Start Time: | am/pm |
| Work Finish Date: | Finish Time: | am/pm |

Is a return visit needed for this job?　　☐ YES　☐ NO

# Return Visit Work

| | | |
|---|---|---|
| Work Start Date: | Start Time: | am/pm |
| Work Finish Date: | Finish Time: | am/pm |

Is a return visit needed for this job?　　☐ YES　☐ NO

| | | |
|---|---|---|
| Work Start Date: | Start Time: | am/pm |
| Work Finish Date: | Finish Time: | am/pm |

Date repair is completed:

Notes / Comments:

# Repairs Log Sheet

| Repair Job No: | Date: |
|---|---|

Name of person reporting repair:

Where is the fault?

Description of fault / repair required:

| Priority given: | ☐ Emergency | ☐ Routine | ☐ 5 working days |
|---|---|---|---|
| | ☐ Urgent | ☐ 24 hours | ☐ 20 working days |

Name of Company doing the work:

Name of person carrying out work:

| Work Start Date: | Start Time: | am/pm |
|---|---|---|
| Work Finish Date: | Finish Time: | am/pm |

| Is a return visit needed for this job? | ☐ YES ☐ NO |
|---|---|

# Return Visit Work

| Work Start Date: | Start Time: | am/pm |
|---|---|---|
| Work Finish Date: | Finish Time: | am/pm |

| Is a return visit needed for this job? | ☐ YES ☐ NO |
|---|---|

| Work Start Date: | Start Time: | am/pm |
|---|---|---|
| Work Finish Date: | Finish Time: | am/pm |

Date repair is completed:

Notes / Comments:

# Repairs Log Sheet

| Repair Job No: | Date: | 📅 |
|---|---|---|

Name of person reporting repair: 👤

Where is the fault? 🔍

Description of fault / repair required:

| Priority given: | ☐ Emergency | ☐ Routine | ☐ 5 working days |
|---|---|---|---|
| | ☐ Urgent | ☐ 24 hours | ☐ 20 working days |

Name of Company doing the work: 🏢

Name of person carrying out work: 🪪

| Work Start Date: | 📅 | Start Time: | am/pm |
|---|---|---|---|
| Work Finish Date: | 📅 | Finish Time: | am/pm |

Is a return visit needed for this job?　　　☐ YES ☐ NO

# Return Visit Work

| Work Start Date: | 📅 | Start Time: | am/pm |
|---|---|---|---|
| Work Finish Date: | 📅 | Finish Time: | am/pm |

Is a return visit needed for this job?　　　☐ YES ☐ NO

| Work Start Date: | 📅 | Start Time: | am/pm |
|---|---|---|---|
| Work Finish Date: | 📅 | Finish Time: | am/pm |

Date repair is completed:

Notes / Comments:

# Repairs Log Sheet

Repair Job No: | Date: 📅

Name of person reporting repair: 👤

Where is the fault? 🔍

Description of fault / repair required:

Priority given: | ☐ Emergency | ☐ Routine | ☐ 5 working days
| ☐ Urgent | ☐ 24 hours | ☐ 20 working days

Name of Company doing the work: 🏢

Name of person carrying out work: 🪪

Work Start Date: 📅 | Start Time: am/pm

Work Finish Date: 📅 | Finish Time: am/pm

Is a return visit needed for this job? ☐ YES ☐ NO

# Return Visit Work

Work Start Date: 📅 | Start Time: am/pm

Work Finish Date: 📅 | Finish Time: am/pm

Is a return visit needed for this job? ☐ YES ☐ NO

Work Start Date: 📅 | Start Time: am/pm

Work Finish Date: 📅 | Finish Time: am/pm

Date repair is completed:

Notes / Comments:

# Repairs Log Sheet

| Repair Job No: | Date: |
|---|---|

Name of person reporting repair:

Where is the fault?

Description of fault / repair required:

| Priority given: | ☐ Emergency | ☐ Routine | ☐ 5 working days |
|---|---|---|---|
| | ☐ Urgent | ☐ 24 hours | ☐ 20 working days |

Name of Company doing the work:

Name of person carrying out work:

| Work Start Date: | Start Time: | am/pm |
|---|---|---|
| Work Finish Date: | Finish Time: | am/pm |

| Is a return visit needed for this job? | ☐ YES ☐ NO |
|---|---|

# Return Visit Work

| Work Start Date: | Start Time: | am/pm |
|---|---|---|
| Work Finish Date: | Finish Time: | am/pm |

| Is a return visit needed for this job? | ☐ YES ☐ NO |
|---|---|

| Work Start Date: | Start Time: | am/pm |
|---|---|---|
| Work Finish Date: | Finish Time: | am/pm |

Date repair is completed:

Notes / Comments:

# Repairs Log Sheet

| Repair Job No: | Date: |
|---|---|

Name of person reporting repair:

Where is the fault?

Description of fault / repair required:

| Priority given: | ☐ Emergency | ☐ Routine | ☐ 5 working days |
|---|---|---|---|
| | ☐ Urgent | ☐ 24 hours | ☐ 20 working days |

Name of Company doing the work:

Name of person carrying out work:

| Work Start Date: | Start Time: | am/pm |
|---|---|---|
| Work Finish Date: | Finish Time: | am/pm |

Is a return visit needed for this job?　　　☐ YES ☐ NO

# Return Visit Work

| Work Start Date: | Start Time: | am/pm |
|---|---|---|
| Work Finish Date: | Finish Time: | am/pm |

Is a return visit needed for this job?　　　☐ YES ☐ NO

| Work Start Date: | Start Time: | am/pm |
|---|---|---|
| Work Finish Date: | Finish Time: | am/pm |

Date repair is completed:

Notes / Comments: